Grand Coulee
Pond Creek
Coulee Lake
a Pond
Rocky Plains
Rocky Country
Falls
Yakima River
Nachas
Emigrant road to Sound from Ft wallawalla
Sandy Plains
33 miles no water
25 miles no water
Wallawalla River
Snake River
Sandy Prairie
Columbia River
Pack trail
Agency
Emigrant Road
Butter creek
Open, Hilly Country

BUGLES IN THE VALLEY

BY H. DEAN GUIE

GARNETT'S FORT SIMCOE

Oregon Historical Society
1977

Published by the Oregon Historical Society
with the aid of the Western Imprints Fund
and the Northwest Area Foundation.

COVER COMPOSITE: Through such rolling hills and prairies, over rocks and across valleys with views of Cascade peaks (here Mt. Adams), Army troops and Indians evaded and confronted each other during the Yakima War that brought Fort Simcoe's beginning. The drawing of Maj. Robert S. Garnett, commander of the post, is by Don Kopp. (Landscape photos by Francis Seufert, Wesley Andrews, OHS Collections.)

TITLE PAGE: Officers row at Fort Simcoe, viewed across the parade ground, 1971. The commanding officer's house, with its gables, is second from right. There Major Garnett brought his bride, Marianna, in May 1857. The other buildings are captains' quarters. (OHS Collections.)

LC 77-088149
SBN 0-87595-057-4

Printed in U.S.A.
Glass-Dahlstrom, Printers
Portland, Oregon

Contents

H.D.G.

Illustrations

MAPS

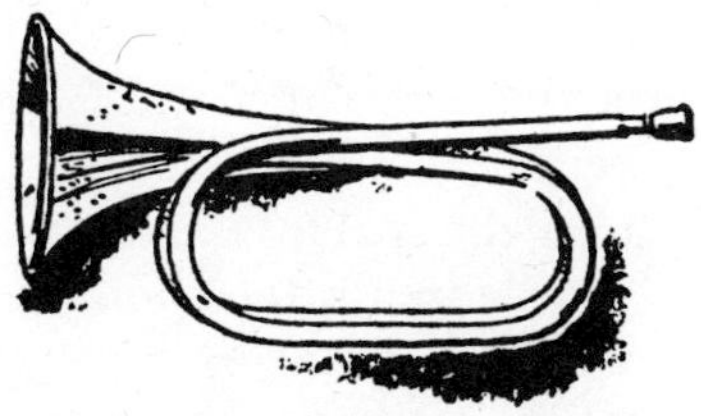

Forward

IN its spacious white oak grove at the head of Simcoe Valley on the Yakima Indian Reservation in south-central Washington, Fort Simcoe graces a bold landscape where bugles of the Ninth Regiment, United States Infantry, first sounded in the summer of 1856. An advance U.S. Army post, 1856-58, subsequently an Indian agency and school, since 1955 it has been a state park under lease from the Yakima Tribe.

Wild flowers in their early blooming season still garnish lavishly the open flats and slopes. The Cascades westward still wear their pines, tamaracks and firs. In the backdrop of a clear sky, snowy Mount Adams (*Pah-toh*—Standing-up) offers its immutable grandeur. Although shut from view at the fort by the immediate foothills, the shapely cone dominates the vast sweep of country and is visible for most of the easterly approach over the gradually rising Toppenish plain. Thereon, farms and pastures, fences and roads have tamed the original aspect, yet not in broad scope. To the south a bit, buttressing the Simcoe Mountains, the bold mass of Toppenish Ridge lifts high the horizon. Northward, bare spurs of the foothills merge with the plain. In such setting the illusion of Fort Simcoe's once real remoteness is strikingly preserved.

When the soldiers came to the land of the confederated Yakima tribes and bands, the site of Fort Simcoe long had been a favorite assembly place for the native people. Main trails from plains and mountains met there, and at this sheltered spot not a few families wintered in circular, mat-roofed, semi-pit houses. Grazing was ample for the horses which the Yakimas possessed in large numbers. Wood was handy and springs ran amid the oaks and willows. One of the springs, rising in the northern part of the grounds, thumped rhythmically. The Indians called it *Mool-Mool,* imitative of its bubbling *(e-moo-lah-cha).* That also was the designation for the camp area and for a local streamlet later named Agency Creek.

Simcoe is derived from the Yakima *Sim-ku-ee* or *Sim-kwee,* the name for a dip or saddle in a ridge about three miles northeast of the fort. It comes from *ku-ee* or *kwee*—spine or back—and *sim*— descriptive of the body's contour, practicularly in the female figure, at the waist.

Simcoe Creek cuts the lower extremity of the ridge, winding from Medicine Valley into the Simcoe Valley on its way to the Toppenish. Simcoe Creek was recorded as *Simkwe* by Brevet Capt. George Brinton McClellan, Corps of Engineers, and as *Simkwee* by Second Lieut. Johnson K. Duncan, Third Artillery, on the 1853 exploring expedition that was part of the great Pacific Railroad northern route reconnaisance under the direction of Washington Territory's first governor, Isaac I. Stevens. Captain McClellan, who twice was to be entrusted with command of the Army of the Potomac, headed the western party of the reconnaisance. Lieutenant Duncan was destined also to become a general but with the Confederacy; he commanded the river defenses below New Orleans when Adm. David Glasgow Farragut took that city. In McClellan's party, Duncan served ably as astronomer, topographer and draftsman.

Starting from Fort Vancouver with his party—numbering 66, including 22 packers and an escort of 28 soldiers—McClellan crossed the Cascades at Klickitat Pass. He dropped into the valley by the *Sahpenis* (Toppenish) Creek trail, and on August 16 made an overnight camp on *Simkwe* Creek. A variation of *Simcoe,* contained in Brevet Maj. Granville O. Haller's accounts of his desperate battle on Toppenish Creek in 1855, is *Sim-coo-a,* in reference to the valley. In some early correspondence from the fort, Simcoe was spelled *Sim-Co-E* and also *Simco.*

In Pacific Northwest history Fort Simcoe has received scant attention from historians, possibly because of its short existence as a military post. The meagerness of published references thus has necessitated rather extensive research. Fortunately, the War Department meticulously saved and stored official correspondence, general and special orders, post returns, muster rolls and other documents—available in the National Archives. Luckily, too, some personal letters and papers have been preserved. While Fort Simcoe's neglect, historically, is lamentable, its relative obscurity otherwise has been all gain. Away from the thoroughfares of progress and development, Simcoe is today, in fair part, as it was over a century ago.

Fort Simcoe's importance is not from battles fought there, for none were, although in the vicinity a lively engagement took place in the year prior to its founding; besides the valid claim on us for its unusual charms, Simcoe has historical significance. It was an advance post in an essential system of military establishments, and figures conspicuous in Northwest, Pacific Coast and national history briefly called it home and drilled on its parade ground. It is a modest monument to the old pre-Civil War regular Army, and particularly to the Ninth Infantry which furnished the garrison. In fact, the story of Fort Simcoe, the military post, as distinguished from that of its later usage, is part of the history of the Ninth when the entire regiment served in Washington and Oregon territories.*

"The Old Regular Army," an accolade recurrently conferred on the Army of the United States, carries with it the qualities of dash, dependability, stamina and fortitude. The Greek phalanxes and the Roman legions, in their centuries, doubtless were similarly and affectionately labeled. To the chroniclers of their deeds and glories, the old armies have been the grand armies, achieving mightily in rigorous and romantic yesterday. The Old Army of the 1850s was, in the classic tradition of historic counterparts, tough, well-officered, proud of its service record. It mustered scarcely 12,000 in 1855 and but some 15,000 in 1856.

*The Ninth Infantry first was established under authority granted to the President on July 16, 1798, to raise 12 regiments of 10 companies each, because of "differences between the United States and the French Republic." Officers were appointed from Maryland and recruiting was done in that state. On the settling of difficulties with France, enlistments were suspended, and the new Ninth was disbanded, June 15, 1800. In 1812 it again was organized and raised in Massachusetts, with that state's Simon Learned as colonel. In 1847 the next regiment of like designation was authorized and recruiting done largely in Rhode Island and Massachusetts. In April, 1848, it was mustered out of service at Fort Adams, Rhode Island. The Ninth Infantry and the Tenth Infantry were "bugle regiments," furnished with bugles instead of drums. From *History of the Ninth U.S. Infantry, 1799-1909,* by Capt. Fred R. Brown (R.R. Donnelley & Sons Co., Chicago, 1909).

The "Old Army" of the nineteenth century as represented in its uniforms, 1855-58, from left: Artillery, Infantry, Mounted Rifles and Light Artillery. Painting by H. A. Ogden, lithographed in New York by G. H. Buek & Co., and copyrighted 1885 by S. B. Holabird, Qr. Master Gen'l U.S.A. (National Archives.)

The greater portion was spread thin on the frontiers and emigrant routes. Senior officers—West Pointers and others—included veterans of the costly Seminole War, the War with Mexico, even that of 1812, and of fighting marches in the West. Some yet to taste battle were on the way to glory and renown.

Men of that stamp put Fort Simcoe on the map and otherwise had a hand in the Pacific Northwest's Indian war of 1855-56 and in the finale of 1858. But not a few then smartly saluting the 32-star flag of the Republic soon would be pledging fealty to another bright bunting, the Stars and Bars of the Confederate States of America. Notably of the latter were Maj. Robert Selden Garnett☆ of Virginia, Fort Simcoe's first commandant, and Capt. James J. Archer☆ of Maryland, who eventually succeeded to command.

The two Southerners, Garnett and Archer, and Capt. Dickinson Woodruff☆ were the chief, on-the-ground figures associated with the building and garrisoning of Simcoe. Their Department of the Pacific commander, Maj. Gen. John Ellis Wool,☆ of Mexican War fame and a hero of 1812, ordered the establishment of the post. Their colonel, George Wright,☆ selected the site and directed Garnett to proceed with construction, of which Woodruff also for a time was in charge. Archer wound up the building job, and, finally, the affairs of the post. Not of the military but most useful to it was Louis Scholl,☆ the supervising architect.

Fort Simcoe was established as a temporary post for both the control and protection of the Indians, whom some of the military believed had been victimized by the territorial governments and likely to be set upon by civilian forces seeking Indian horses and cattle and vengeance for attacks on white settlers and travelers in 1855-56. In the first year of construction and on Major Garnett's recommendation it was classified a permanent post. Despite a ceasing of hostilities in 1856, the prospect seemed to be a long need for a firm hand. So extra-duty men of the Ninth Infantry and mechanics hired by the Quartermaster's Department built the fort to last, at an estimated cost of $35,000.

When war flared anew in 1858—with the Palouses, Spokanes, Coeur d'Alenes comprising the bulk of the hostiles but with a few Yakimas participating—the military took such effective

☆Indicates biographical sketch in "Among Those Present . . ."

Captain's quarters at Ft. Simcoe in agency period, with picket fence and board walks. (H. D. Guie photo.)

action that the tribes soon were humbled to amenable wards. Simcoe hardly was completed before its usefulness as a military post was ended. But, a valuable property, it was well located for an agency for the Yakimas. The Army turned it over to the Bureau of Indian Affairs, and in May of 1859 the last company of the garrison marched out. For six decades, until the agency was moved to Toppenish in 1923, Fort Simcoe was the place where civil employees of the government administered the business of the reservation, taught husbandry and instructed the children and grandchildren of warriors, hunters and fishermen. The remaining "Old Mool-Mool boys and girls" have fond recollections of their years at the agency school, although in the beginning they were not easily persuaded that it was advisable or necessary to learn from books and to become proficient in trades such as carpentry, blacksmithing and in farming, or for the girls to become familiar with a newer style of housekeeping.

Notable of the early agents was the iron-willed, big, athletic James Harvey Wilbur, once of New York City, and pioneer Oregon Methodist Episcopal minister and missionary. Father Wilbur, as all knew him, founded the agency school in 1861. President Lincoln appointed him agent of the reservation in 1864, and following a short military administration he was re-

The Rev. James H. Wilbur, Methodist missionary and 1847 Oregon pioneer, was born in New York, died in 1877 at Walla Walla. Wife was Lucretia Ann Stevens. They went to Simcoe when Wilbur was appointed Superintendent of Education on the Yakima Reservation, 1860. As Indian agent and in other capacities, he served the reservation for 20 years. (OHS Collections.)

turned as the agent in 1871. For 20 years the Reverend Wilbur and his dedicated wife exerted a strong civilizing influence.

During the agency period, with the agents and staff occupying the former officers quarters, the post lost its military atmosphere. The parade ground was plowed and planted as a garden, tended by boys of the school, and then, in 1861, as an orchard. Various of the military buildings were razed and replaced by frame structures. Three of the square-log blockhouses disappeared; that at the southeastern corner of the quadrangle was long used as an icehouse and finally chopped for firewood. In 1949, fire destroyed the last of the barracks, that of Company I, and the storehouse and subsistence storehouse of Army days, at the southeastern angle of the parade.

The first attempt to preserve Fort Simcoe, in the autumn of 1938 under the auspices of the Bureau of Indian Affairs, was at the instance of Mrs. Frederick (Ethel) Swanstrom, Seattle, Society of Colonial Dames. L. V. McWhorter, of Yakima, Northwest Indian lore and war historian long trusted by Yakima tribal leaders, helped to get the Indians' approval of the project.

That initial restoration enterprise was conducted with labor supplied from an Indian conservation corps forestry unit quartered in the old school buildings, and it was going along nicely until the outbreak of World War II ended all CCC activity. Due to that work—the repairing of some foundations and floors, reshingling of roofs and repainting of exteriors—the four resi-

Southwest blockhouse. (H. D. Guie photo.)

dences comprising officers row were still in surprisingly good condition when the Washington State Parks and Recreation Commission took charge 12 years later and instituted a second restoration program. But the last of the blockhouses—squatting on a sagebrush rise off the southwest point of the quadrangle—was an almost roofless shell. The young conservation corps men did not have time to make repairs to the blockhouse, to which Mr. McWhorter contributed the last roof, but they restored the parade ground, clearing it of the neglected agency orchard.

Under the parks commission program to restore Simcoe to its general appearance as a military post, agency era buildings were razed and attention was given to repairing original structures and rebuilding others in accordance with contemporary sketches and data. Work was begun in September 1953, under the Direction of Albert Culverwell, parks historian.

In March, 1953, the parks commission and the Yakima Tribal Council effected a 25-year, renewable lease for 140 acres of the site, designated Fort Simcoe Historical State Park. In 1955, with the authority of an Act of Congress, the tribe leased the property and 60 adjoining acres to the state for 99 years. The enabling legislation, jointly requested by the tribal council and the Fort Simcoe at Mool-Mool Restoration Society, was authored by Congressman O. H. "Hal" Holmes and unanimously supported by the Washington congressional delegation. The society was formed in Yakima in 1952 to foster continuing interest in restoration. Participants in the proceedings recall that the state adoption of Fort Simcoe for restoration was primarily projected by Mrs. Ruth E. Peeler, parks commission vice chairman.

BUGLES IN THE VALLEY

Major Robert Selden Garnett, U.S.A., as he appeared in the later 1850s when he directed construction of and commanded Fort Simcoe. After the deaths of his wife and child there he returned East. Later he became a brigadier general for the Confederacy and was killed in battle in 1861. (National Archives.)

"'Bring No Ploughs'"

THE grand treaty council in the Walla Walla Valley, 130 miles south and east of Mool-Mool, May 29-June 9, 1855, led incidentally, if not directly, to the Yakima War and the establishing of Fort Simcoe. Governor Isaac I. Stevens, as superintendent of Indian affairs for Washington Territory, and Gen. Joel Palmer, superintendent of such affairs for Oregon Territory, jointly conducted the council, which Stevens dominated.

Stevens had managed easily in treating with tribes of the Puget Sound region. With the horseback tribes he had to extend his persuasive powers. He was in a hurry to extinguish native claims to large areas that he foresaw soon would be sought by settlers. The Indians were in no hurry. They wanted to deliberate the proposals. Chief Kamiakin, his aging relative, Chief Owhi, and his younger brother, Chief Skloom, of the Yakimas, were especially reluctant to deal. Hammering away, Stevens prevailed, and 11 days after the formal convening of the council, the leaders of the 5,000 Indians assembled for the momentous occasion affixed their marks to documents ceding most of the country used and occupied by the tribes to the United States.

Three treaties were made—with the historically friendly and powerful Nez Perces, with the Walla Wallas and Umatillas and their neighbors, the Cayuses of Marcus Whitman massacre ill repute, and with the tribes and bands designated for convenience by Stevens as the "Yakima Nation." That "nation" numbered an estimated 3,900 persons. The namesake tribe, the Yakimas, totaling about 700, had its abode in the Yakima Valley, which it shared with some closely related bands. By the three treaties the government gained title to some 60,000 square miles in the present states of Idaho, Oregon and Washington. The Yakima confederation ceded 16,920 square miles (10,828,800 acres) for $200,000 and retained 1,875 square miles (1,200,000 acres) for a reservation.

Before the council the Yakimas had seemed well enough disposed, although there had been occasional rumors and reports of plottings to unite the Northwestern tribes in war. In 1853 the Yakimas had not objected to Captain McClellan's explorations nor to the passage of the first emigrant train through their country, on the route from the Hudson's Bay Company's old Fort Walla Walla through Naches Pass to Steilacoom on Puget Sound. They had been friendly to traders and tolerated prospectors panning for gold in the Cascade streams. For the Catholic priests at St. Joseph Mission on Ahtanum Creek they had respect and in them reposed confidence. Kamiakin, who was to become a leading spirit in the war, had a house and garden near the mission. But by 1853 they were growing uneasy over the increasing westward migration which skirted their country, and they were disturbed by the not infrequent clashes between settlers and Indians in southern Oregon and northern California.

In the spring of 1853 a delegation of Yakima, Cayuse and Walla Walla chiefs had visited Capt. Benjamin Alvord, Fourth Infantry, commanding the little post of Fort Dalles on the Columbia River. They told him that they welcomed "gentlemen, Hudson Bay Company men or officers of the Army, or engineers" to their country, and did not object to persons merely hunting or wearing swords, but that they "dreaded the approach of whites with ploughs, axes, and shovels in their hands." That expression of sentiment, added to information he had received from priests at the Ahtanum mission, alarmed the captain. He promptly informed Governor Stevens "of these threatened Indian difficulties, and of the gigantic scale of their proposed insurrection."

If such an insurrection were brewing, the treaties insisted upon by Stevens at Walla Walla, where Chief Kamiakin had voiced resentment over the proceedings, apparently hastened the outbreak. While the treaties were not obligatory until confirmed by the Senate, which was not done until 1859, no time was lost in announcing that the ceded areas were open to settlement. Official notices appeared over the names of Stevens and

Massachusetts-born Isaac I. Stevens graduated as top cadet from West Point in 1839. After the Mexican War (he was brevetted major) he was in charge of a branch of the Pacific Railroad Survey. He led Federal troops in the Civil War and was killed in 1862. (OHS Collections.)

Palmer in the territorial newspapers in July, a week after those publications had carried reports of gold discoveries in the Colville region of northern Washington Territory. The news started a rush for the diggings by way of The Dalles and the Naches and Snoqualmie passes. The gold hunters disregarded warnings from the Yakimas to stay out.

From the Walla Walla council grounds Governor Stevens and party—22 in all—traveled to the easterly reaches of the territory to treat with the Coeur d'Alenes, Flatheads, Blackfoot and others. While Stevens was there busied, the Yakima War began, touching off hostilities also west of the Cascades. Two days out of Fort Benton, on October 29, on his return journey to the capital at Olympia, the governor received the dismaying intelligence from his intrepid expressman, W. H. Pearson. The latter, bearing dispatches from Olympia, had ridden from The Dalles, using relays of horses, and had barely outdistanced pursuers in the Umatilla Valley.

Pearson reported that the governor's agent to the Yakimas, Andrew J. Bolon, had been murdered in the Simcoe Mountains, that Maj. Granville O. Haller☆ had been whipped in the Simcoe Valley, that all the Walla Walla treaty tribes with the exception of the Nez Perces were openly at war, and that the Puget Sound Indians had attacked the settlements—all taken as evidence of a widespread conspiracy. From Olympia officials Pearson brought letters urging Stevens to descend the Missouri and make a circuitous but safer journey by way of the Isthmus of Panama to the capital. Rejecting that advice, the governor determined to

☆Indicates biographical sketch in "Among Those Present . . ."

retrace his route, regardless of hazards, a feat he signally accomplished, arriving at Olympia on January 19, 1856.

The unfortunate Bolon, Clark County representative in the first territorial legislature, 1854, was large and athletic, with striking red hair and beard. He was well known to the Yakimas. He had been among them to arrange for their appearance at the Walla Walla council and he had been at the council. Hearing reports of the killing of several Puget Sound residents traveling through the Yakima country to the gold strikes near the Hudson's Bay Company post, Fort Colville, he left The Dalles in early September, 1855, to quiz his charges. Riding alone, to show his confidence in them, he had gone to the Catholic mission on Ahtanum Creek, where he hoped to find Kamiakin. The latter was not at home. It was said that the chief avoided him and that Skloom told Bolon there had been a war council in the Grande Ronde Valley, Oregon, but that he, Skloom, had spoken against war.

Returning over the Simcoes, Bolon fell in with a small party of Yakimas. According to historical accounts, these Indians had been pursuing him. But an eyewitness named Su-el-lil (subsequently known as Yakima George) who was about 14 years old, many years later revealed to L. V. McWhorter of Yakima that Bolon overtook the party, consisting of six men, several women and himself, Su-el-lil, and traveled with it. When they stopped at a spring and built a fire to dry out, as the day was dismally wet, Bolon was pinioned and his throat cut. The instigator of the crime was Mosheel, a son of Bolon's good friend, Showawai Kotiaken, also called Ice. Upon hearing of the deed, Ice is said to have cried.

A member of the Indian party reported the slaying to The Dalles. Nathan Olney, Indian agent there, already had sent a Des Chutes Indian to ascertain why Bolon, who had expected to back in three days, was overdue. The spy confirmed the report of the murder and said that Kamiakin had confided his intention to go to war. Olney learned, too, by letter from the Rev. John Baptist Abraham Brouillet, of the mission, that Yakimas had been talking war ever since the Walla Walla council.

The military strength of the Columbia-Puget Sound district was two companies of the Fourth Infantry and one company of the Third Artillery at Fort Vancouver, two companies of the

In October 1855 Major Haller went north from this point on the Columbia toward Mt. Adams and battle beginning on Toppenish Creek. A few hectic days later he made a hurried retreat. Only a few Ft. Dalles roofs show (central) in this 1867 Watkins photo. Town at extreme right, with Columbia River flowing west into the Gorge below Mount Adams. (OHS Collections.)

Fourth at Fort Steilacoom, and two companies of the Fourth and a detachment of dragoons at Fort Dalles.

Major Gabriel James Rains at Fort Vancouver ordered Major Haller from Fort Dalles to the Yakima country, also Lieut. William A. Slaughter and detachment from Fort Steilacoom, by the Naches Pass route, to rendezvous at the mission. Haller was hardly returned from summer patrol of the Oregon Trail to the Salmon Falls of the Snake and punishing perpetrators of the Massacre of a small emigrant party the previous year. He shot some, hung others—three over the graves of their victims at the Hudson's Bay Company old Fort Boise—"as many warriors as they had killed of the white," he said. The toll was 19. The executions, at the direction of the commanding officer, Columbia River and Puget Sound District, were "in hopes" of preventing other murders, said Haller, not for revenge. "The poor

Granville O. Haller, Colonel U.S.A., retired, and prominent Pacific Northwesterner, was a major in 1855 when his military encounter with Indians near Toppenish Creek more or less 'began' the Yakima War. (OHS Collections.)

Indians cannot and should not be judged by the standard of the civilized and Christianized nations of the earth,'' he told the troops in an order requiring ''the utmost decorum'' at the Fort Boise hangings.

At The Dalles Haller mounted up a fresh command, largely of 100 recent recruits, in two companies, crossed the Columbia and marched north early in October 1855. Seasoned Capt. David A. Russell and 2nd Lieut. Archibald Gracie, Jr., both of the late campaign, shared responsibilities of subordinate command. Medical officer was Assistant Surgeon John F. Hammond —rifle, pistol and kit. From the Snake expedition were the essential Sgt. Rowland Cotton, as acting sergeant major, and Sgt. James B. Mulholland, acting commissary sergeant. Of the force but injuring himself at the start of the march, Lieut. St. Clair Dearing reluctantly went back to the post.

Gracie, West Point '54, New York born, appointed from New Jersey, and attached from the Fifth Infantry, had charge of the mountain howitzer, its corporal and ten privates. Sharp soldier, Gracie was soon—in '56—to chuck the uniform and turn cotton factor at Mobile. He'd join in the rebellion of the seceding states and, a brigadier at 32, fall in the trenches before Petersburg, December 3, 1864.

Cutmouth John, Cayuse, also known as Cayuse John, rode happy in his moccasins, jogging at the head of the column, ranging for long looks, reining beside the commander, to whom he had taken a fancy in '54 when Haller was scouting Oregon's Grande Ronde. John enrolled as guide for a whack at the Snakes and stayed for more campaigns, proving himself, said Haller, ''invaluable, always faithful.'' His catchy sobriquet derived from a bullet wound in the Cayuse War, in which trouble he was not with the bad Indians.

Brought along to try out was a new long-range rifle with a supply of Minie balls. Opportunity offered, about 3 p.m., October 6, fourth day from the Columbia, as the advance scuffed the last stony terrace from the Simcoes to the crossing of bluff-edged, oak and cottonwood-fringed Toppenish Creek. Appearing on a high point, a chiefly, gesticulating figure presented a fair target. The new rifle's custodian let fly and missed, sounding, said Haller, ''the tocsin of war,'' echoed by whoops and gunfire from the woody bottom, where flitting ambushers

Top left shows rocky (west) part of Haller hill position, first afternoon, looking east. Top right also looks east from part of Haller field first afternoon. Lower right view of trenched sandy knoll (center) of Haller field, first day; view east. (All H. D. Guie photos, 1954.)
In lower left photo view is to east from second day field of Haller battle on Toppenish Creek. Twiwash, "Last Warrior," points up slope, west. In background are Indian farms along creek. (L. V. McWhorter photo, Oct. 18, 1921, from about center of battlefield.)

were harangued to stand firm for reinforcement by Kamiakin—so packer Donald McKay interpreted.

Howitzer off the mules in a jiffy, Gracie threw spherical case into the cover, the racket hurrying the rear guard with the pack train. Starting with skirmishers down the reach to the ford, Sgt. James C. Roper of C Company found himself unsupported, got back with two minor arm wounds. Corporal McGarvey of I Company fared better with his squad, killing an Indian aiming at a soldier.

Scoopings in a pair of sandy knolls and several heapings of scab rock still mark the troop position. For horses and mules there was a swale. Over the copse on the Toppenish the view north went far, elsewhere was limited by high ground. At the east or right, within musket range, a wedge-shaped bluff (Haller's description) was used to effect by the foe, prevented by skirmishers from occupying the hill in back of the command, whose left had the vantage of sharp, basaltic pitches to the streamside.

Captain Russell filtered many of his company undetected down the foliaged steep bank on his front, flanking the enemy front and rear. A general advance scoured the 200 or more warriors out of the brush at dusk and from the fight. Collecting its eight wounded—one fatally, one badly—and one dead, the battalion moved north in the dark about a mile from its first position, crossing an open flat and groping up a draw to a safer location on a far-running slope With Indians continuing in evidence, the command slept on its arms.

Daylight yielded generous prospects, including the hill of yesterday's stand. Not quite in sight, northwest, was the Yakimas' resort of Mool-Mool. Also on the far side of a ridge twelve miles north was the Ahtanum mission and close-by home of Chief Kamiakin. Haller had abandoned the idea of going to the mission.

The position occupied part of an ancient burial ground, indicated by rings and heapings of lava rock and particularly noted by Haller on stationing a small group at a low, eastward facing bluff with graves on top and in the sliderock. Within his 400-yard perimeter of defense is the present Colwash Cemetery, fenced and with headstones. (Several Columbia River Wascos of the Chief Colwash band were employed by the Army and the family name long has been on the rolls of the Yakima Reservation.)

Cutmouth John, Cayuse, "Always faithful," Haller said, but Sheridan in 1856 felt John's actions lowered the expedition's tone. (H.D. Guie Collection.)

Defensible as was the sloping terrain of scattered hillocks, sandy spots and stony outcroppings, Sunday dawned an anxious day. Indians opened fire at sunup, and through the early hours horseback warriors and spectators swarmed from the Ahtanum, lower Toppenish, Mool-Mool and Medicine Valley. Relatively few of the assembled host of Yakimas and friends—estimated as high as 1,500—had guns but some owned rifles far outranging the infantry smoothbores and, Haller put in his journal that day, "of surprising accuracy." The Indians, he said, "make good shots at half a mile off and the balls are troublesome." He recorded, too, that the new, long range rifle was of "little account," fouling at each discharge by lead left in the grooves and thus hard to reload. The fault was the too-thin casing of the Minie ball. He expressed concern over the recruits wasting ammunition, banging "eternally without aim or mark," and relief that he and Captain Russell each brought 500 or 600 rounds in addition to the issue of 40 per man. "I am thinking of retreat," he said, "before a retreat becomes impracticable," and wrote a letter to be carried at first chance to Fort Dalles, summoning 1st Lieut. Edward H. Day, Third Artillery.

Bayonet and howitzer were saving the bacon, plugging gaps in the undermanned ring of defense, extended to better protect the wounded, the mules and the horses. Without graze and water some of the animals had strayed to enemy hands. Some were lost in the night move to the hill. The howitzer early in the attack scattered a concentration pressing Russell on the west. Thereafter merely wheeling the consternating twelve-pounder to a threatened sector usually sufficed. It could be devastating at 150 yards.

Sergeant Mulholland, Corporal McGarvey, Lance Corporal McIntosh and Private Wilson of I Company showed holders of the perimeter points how to clear ground with the bayonet. Such demonstrations sent skirmishers scampering and inclined the besiegers to contend behind impromptu stone breastworks at rifle range. Their shortage of guns was a handicap but by trading back and forth some could rest while others maintained the fire.

By late afternoon weary recruits were conjuring foes creeping in shadowed spots and waving grass, and would send for the major, who would remain with them and chat, he wrote, "until their minds were delivered of the danger." At sunset the spectators vacated their vantage points, warriors their positions, all departing in dusty cavalcades. They'd finish the fight tomorrow. The Fourth's losses in the two days were two dead, Privates Herman and Regan, who were buried on the field, and thirteen wounded. Indian casualties were undetermined; last warriors years later said they were extremely light.

Haller reconnoitered and packed up fast. The thirsty command watered at the Toppenish, ascended and crossed the ground of the initial stand and, in darkness so thick that Cutmouth John got down often to feel the way, climbed Toppenish Ridge by the Eel Trail, the steep, zigzagging *Ahsoom* or *Assum* of native legend. The 40-man rear guard mistakenly followed a tangent route in the gloom and was not thereafter a factor. Its absence was felt when pursuit overtook the advance section of 60 men, including the wounded, the next morning.

In a running fight for several miles, the overnight veterans kept the enemy at such length that but two of the soldiers were struck and Cutmouth John could take off unnoticed on Haller's fast *Selim* for The Dalles, 50 miles—eight hours—away. When the mule carrying the brass howitzer barrel could no longer stagger, the piece was cached in the dry bed of a small stream and covered with cottonwood leaves. Gaining a high prairie patch of pine, which the Indians tried to burn, the unit held, cared for the wounded and animals and cleaned its firearms.

By 4 p.m. the enemy had some "good positions" in the woods, said Haller, "and were doing some execution." He and Russell led bayonet charges and the attackers fled, but in that final clash Sergeant Mulholland received a third and fatal wound and Private Bremen fell. The Indians built fires at discreet distance, as if to illumine the vicinity and discourage resumption of the retreat, begun at sundown—packs jettisoned so that all the remaining mules served as mounts.

At the end of the night march the missing rear guard was found encamped and wondering why its own forced marching had not enabled it to catch up. Met by Lieutenant Day's reinforcing Company L, the reunited command arrived on the tenth at Fort Dalles. Campaign casualties were five killed and 17 wounded, some twice. Sergeant Mulholland's body was carried to the fort, and into the record went Haller's tribute to "a very gallant and worthy soldier," whose conduct throughout was "conspicuous and distinguished." All the noncommissioned officers "behaved most gallantly." The two first sergeants and two lance corporals each were wounded. Sergeant Cotton of K found in his breast pocket an enemy ball lodged in one of his rifle balls.

Praising his officers, the major mentioned that Dr. Hammond "bestowed every care" possible on the wounded and "also found opportunities to shoot," there being little doubt on four occasions that "he killed and wounded his mark." The men in the ranks, he said, "behaved with courage and energy, particularly after they had become accustomed to the war whoop and the crack of the rifle." With soldierly generosity, Haller summed up: "In regard to the enemy before us, it is due them to say that they fought with a courage far beyond my expectations and continued their efforts without intermission for such a protracted period as to suggest unpleasant ideas."

Feeling "answerable" for the "considerable" losses of public property—30 mules, the commissary supplies abandoned or destroyed, and particularly the howitzer—Haller requested a court of inquiry to determine if he had taken "sufficient pains" to preserve the same, but the Department of the Pacific had more pressing business. Surely, he would not have been censured for sacrificing stores so that the pack mules could carry the wounded and well, otherwise afoot, nor for feeding flour to the hungry, weakened animals, nor for distributing as much bread and sugar as each man could manage on the night march from the scene of the last encounter.

Lieutenant Slaughter on the Naches Pass road with 40 of the Steilacoom garrison learned from a scout of Haller's check and judiciously withdrew.

In November, 1915, Su-el-lil guided historian McWhorter and interpreter William Charley, horseback, from White Swan on the Yakima Reservation to the Bolon murder place, Wahkshum Spring. Severity of the weather permitted little tarrying. Su-el-lil died the following year. In May, 1917, McWhorter and Charley, again horseback, returned to further examine the site in the northwest corner of Sec. 24, T6, R15, Klickitat County, and just south of the reservation line. On October 6, 1918, the Washington State Historical Society, of which McWhorter was a member, dedicated two markers—a granite block near the spring and a granite slab monument to Bolon in the southwest quarter of Sec. 3, T5, R15, near the intersection of Cedar Valley Road and Yaekel Trail, 11 miles northwest of Goldendale. Among speakers at the ceremony was Governor Stevens' ailing 76-year-old son, General Hazard Stevens, society vice president, who as a boy of 12 years knew Bolon in Olympia. His speech hardly begun, Stevens collapsed. He died five days later in Goldendale.

Lieut. Lyman Bissell prepared a topographical map of Colonel Wright's operations in the Yakima country in 1856, which Wright forwarded to Department of the Pacific headquarters with a letter dated May 15, 1857. Wright also reports the establishment of Fort Simcoe and reconnaissance of the route north from Fort Dalles so that six-mule wagons could carry supplies to the new post most of the year. (National Archives, RG 98, Dept. of Pacific, Letters Received; map RG 77.)

Everything but a Battle

ASSEMBLING disposable troops of the Fourth Infantry and Third Artillery and a detachment of dragoons under Second Lieut. Philip H. Sheridan,* Maj. Gabriel J. Rains left The Dalles on October 30, 1855. His command consisted of about 350 regulars and two companies of Washington Volunteers mustered into the federal service from Clark and King counties. He was accompanied by four companies of mounted Oregon Volunteers independently commanded by Col. James W. Nesmith, later a United States senator from Oregon. The combined forces numbered 700.

Charles H. Mason, acting governor of Washington Territory during the absence of Governor Stevens from the capital, visited Rains at Camp Yakima, opposite The Dalles, and conferred the rank of brigadier general of the Washington militia. Sheridan called that a bit of "hocus-pocus."

Sheridan—for the spicing of the history of the campaign—had arrived opportunely at Portland on October 9. With his 18 dragoons, he had escorted a railroad topographical survey party up through Oregon. He was comfortably encamped near Fort Vancouver when word of Haller's defeat was brought down the Columbia by the little sidewheeler *Belle* of Oregon City, and was pressed into service by Rains.

Major (or Brig. Gen.) Rains took the long route to the objective point, the Ahtanum mission, marching to the lower Yakima Valley instead of across the Simcoes. The expedition covered only eight miles in the first three days, as the civilian packers had refused to mount guard over the pack animals and there were many strays to be rounded up. Early in the morning of

November 3, Indians ran off 25 horses and five mules. Skirmishing along the Yakima River resulted in the drowning of two soldiers attempting to ford the stream and the wounding of two Oregon Volunteers.

About 2 o'clock in the afternoon of November 9 the hostiles were found collected in some force at Two Buttes (at Union Gap) which the Indians called *Pah-quy-ti-koot* (Mountain-heads-coming-together). Sheridan proposed that he charge with his dragoons through the river gap while infantry made a flanking attack up the west butte. Rains refused the suggestion, and camp was pitched out of range of the Indians' "desultory fire, but near enough," says Sheridan in his memoirs, "to observe plainly their menacing and tantalizing exhibitions of contempt." A few ineffective rounds were fired from the howitzers. The taunting, Sheridan relates, finally so aggravated the regulars and volunteers "that between 3 and 4 o'clock in the afternoon, by an inexplicable concert of action, and with a serious breach of discipline, a large number of the men and many of the officers broke *en masse* from the camp with loud yells and charged the offending savages."

Among the officers in that rush were Major Haller and Capt. Christopher C. Augur. The latter would become a major general in command of the Washington, D.C., Department troops—the Twenty-second Corps (1863-65)—and be in charge of the search for the conspirators involved in the assassination of Abraham Lincoln.

"The hill," Sheridan goes on, "was readily taken by this unmilitary proceeding, and no one was hurt on either side, but as Rains would not permit it to be held, a large bonfire was lighted on the crest in celebration of the victory, and then all hands marched back to camp, where they had no sooner arrived and got settled down than the Indians returned to the summit of the ridge, seemingly to enjoy the fire that had been so generously built for their benefit, and with renewed taunts and gestures continued to insult us."

At daylight the Army started a systematic advance. Sheridan's dragoons led the main body through the gap and three infantry companies moved up the ridge. The Indians dispersed so quickly that none except an old man on a lame horse and carrying a useless Hudson's Bay pistol remained in sight when the column

"Little Phil" Sheridan, successful and audacious Union Army commander during the Civil War and major general, was second lieutenant in Fourth Infantry with Major Rains' 1855 Yakima expedition. Sheridan was prominent in relief of the Cascades after the attack there in the spring of 1856. (OHS Collections.)

debouched into the upper valley. The lone ancient was killed and scalped by the command's Indian guide, Cutmouth John.

The troops that evening camped near the mission, there to await a small column from Fort Steilacoom under Capt. Maurice Maloney, Fourth Infantry, due by way of the Naches Pass.

"Next morning," Sheridan relates, "the first thing I saw when I put my head out from my blankets was 'Cut-mouth John,' already mounted and parading himself through the camp. The scalp of the Indian he had despatched the day before was tied to the cross-bar of his bridle bit, the hair dangling almost to the ground, and John was decked out in the sacred vestments of Father Pandoza, having, long before anyone was stirring in the camp, ransacked the log-cabin at the Mission in which the good man had lived. John was at all times a most repulsive looking individual, a part of his mouth having been shot away in a fight . . . some years before . . . but his revolting appearance was now worse than ever, and the sacrilegious use of Father Pandoza's vestments, coupled with the ghastly scalp that hung from his bridle, so turned opinion against him that he was soon captured, dismounted, and his parade brought to an abrupt close, and I doubt whether he ever after quite reinstated himself in the good graces of the command."

The untenanted mission, which Sheridan describes as a "comfortable log-house," and which Colonel Nesmith mentions as a "pole and log hut," was burned by Oregon Volunteers. The excuse was that the absent priest, the Rev. J. Charles Pandosy, had been supplying gunpowder to the Indians. A half-keg of powder was unearthed in the vegetable garden by men digging for potatoes. Nesmith says that the building was "accidently burned." Sheridan says a "large heap of dry wood was collected and piled in the building, matches applied," and the mission, which included the priests' quarters, destroyed before the officers in camp were aware of what was going on.

House and chapel first were looted by regulars and volunteers despite an alleged or rumored order by Major Rains that nothing but vegetables be taken. Rains himself was there, Haller said he was told, "giving directions." At his own camp about two miles below the mission, Haller heard that Capt. E.O.C. Ord☆ had a party at the mission picking up things and presently saw Ord's pack animals pass with "lots of bags" and a buffalo robe, and

"Captain Wallen's man, Brooke, with the padre's hat on that shuts up with spring hinges," and at headquarters "some ten chickens laying there dead." By that time Haller thought he should send a party for vegetables but early comers had reaped the harvest. A Roman Catholic of his command deposited in the major's tent "a great many pictures, crucifixes, etc.," said Haller, "to be turned over to Father Mesplie at The Dalles. I amused myself assorting them and packing them up."

Among the mission items was a Yakima language dictionary by Father Pandosy. It would go to George Gibbs, geologist, ethnologist and primarily surveyor with Governor Stevens' western exploration and participant in the treaty councils. (His *Dictionary of the Chinook Jargon* was published in 1863.) In correspondence with Major Haller, Father Pandosy asked that his dictionary be returned. While the mission was going up in smoke, some of the volunteers were catching up the best of the Indian horses lately brought in and shooting the worthless. Indian beef just off the hoof was distributed.

No news being received from Captain Maloney, and fearing that he might be surrounded by Indians at the pass, Rains sent Sheridan and the dragoons and Nesmith with 250 mounted volunteers to the rescue. They rode out in a light snowfall over the Indian trail to the Naches River and up the valley to what Sheridan calls the "eastern mouth" of the pass. As they proceeded, the fall grew heavy and presently the horses could plod no further. They retraced their route to an abandoned Indian village and bivouacked for the night. In the morning, Sheridan, who had pulled an Indian mat over him, found himself under two feet of snow, "from which I arose with difficulty, yet grateful that it had kept me warm during the night."

Rightly concluding, after hardbread and coffee, that Maloney had met with similar difficulties and had camped somewhere on the Naches trail and had no more chance of reaching them than they had of getting to him, the two officers took their commands back to the mission.

With the Indians evidently far out of the country and the snowstorm continuing, Rains started for The Dalles by the "short route" to and across the Simcoes. Nesmith's battalion broke trail, followed by the dragoons, infantry and artillery with its three howitzers. On November 15 the already weary expedition encamped at Haller's battlefield on Toppenish Creek. Examining the position Haller occupied in his defense, Nesmith deemed it surprising that he had escaped with a single man. "The courage and intrepidity displayed by the major and his command," the colonel comments in a report to Gov. George Law Curry of Oregon Territory, "is worthy of the highest commendation."

With Capt. Absalom J. Hembree, Oregon Volunteers, and others, Haller revisited the field later that day and found that the remains of Privates Herman and Regan had been dug up and scattered by coyotes or wolves. Collecting, he said, "the skulls and spinal columns and some few bones," he took them to the headquarters camp for burial with funeral honors. "They were interred just at twilight and Maj. Rains read the burial services when the escort fired three volleys over the graves."

On the eighteenth the expedition reached the Klickitat Valley where the jaded horses, for some days on scant forage, again had grass. In fact, before the departure from the mission, many of the animals, Nesmith relates, were so worn down that they were shot rather than to abandon them to the Indians.

It had been, indeed, a rather perilous passage and it could have ended disastrously. At the summit of the range, Nesmith's guides had become confused and taken the wrong route across the plateau, six feet deep with snow. Sheridan's Scot-Indian guide, Donald McKay, who knew the country, discovered the advance battalion's mistake but some time was lost before Nesmith could be reached and recalled. "The deep snow," Sheridan tells, "made our work extremely laborious, exhausting men and horses almost to the point of relinquishing the struggle, but our desperate situation required that we should get down into the valley beyond, or run the chance of perishing on the mountain in a storm which seemed unending. About midnight the column reached the valley, very tired and hungry, but much elated over its escape."

The expedition had an amusing footnote. Safely back at Fort Dalles, "almost everyone," in Sheridan's words, voted it a "wretched failure," with Rains scattering "far and wide blame for the failure of his combinations," and various of his officers placing the fault on Rains. The wrangling led to the preferring of charges of incompetency against the major by Captain Ord.

"Rains met the charges," says Sheridan, "with counter-charges against Ord, whom he accused of purloining Father Pandoza's shoes, when the soldiers in their fury about the ammunition destroyed the Mission. At the time of its destruction a rumor of this nature was circulated through the camp, started by some wag, no doubt in jest; for Ord, who was somewhat eccentric in his habits, and had started on the expedition rather indifferently shod in carpet-slippers, here came out in a brand-new pair of shoes. Of course there was no real foundation for such a report, but Rains was not above small things, as the bringing of this petty accusation attests."

A letter sent by Ord to the *New York Herald* and published on February 17, 1856, said, in part: "Our expedition went into the Yakima country some 800 strong, about 500 volunteers and 300 regulars. A big fight was expected but the commanding officer of the regulars was by nature adapted for anything but a partisan chief. He marched about over plains and mountains, got into rivers, drowned some men, lost a lot of horses and mules, got into snows, marshes and every type of scrape except a battle (though there was some chance of it) lost some of his party, burned a Catholic mission and then came in with about the most disgusted set of young army officers and volunteers that we have seen lately. No doubt the chief's report to Washington states that the expedition had produced a great moral effect. No young officer is asked for a true report and so that the truth is not told, it is considered unmilitary to write to the papers to tell the truth 'out of school.' So much for fogy field officers and, dear people, you have got hardly any others. The field officers of all the regiments except perhaps the recently created where young men are put in are all old fogies. . . ."

In those days there was no clearing with the Pentagon.

Among others, Haller also felt Rains' spleen. He, too, had written to a newspaper, the *Oregonian,* at Portland, giving an account of his own unsuccessful invasion of the Yakima country, before making his official report. For that offense and for his "shameful retreat" and abandonment of his mountain howitzer, Haller found charges lodged against him.

Nothing ever came of the cases, as Maj. Gen. John Ellis Wool,* department commander, considered Rains' charges trivial, and did not have enough officers of proper rank to constitute a court to try Rains.

Maj. Gen. Edward O. C. Ord had a long military career including the Seminole War, California during the Mexican War, Rains' later acrimonious 1855 expedition (Ord was captain), the Rogue River War in 1856, Wright's 1858 campaign, command of Fort Vancouver early in 1861, and distinguished Civil War service. (National Archives.)

In accordance with General Wool's verbal directions, 1st Lieut. Robert Macfeely, acting assistant quartermaster, Fort Vancouver, reported the number of animals lost on the expedition. Of the 344 taken on the campaign, the loss, he said, was 48 horses and 10 mules. Three horses and one mule, unable to travel further, were abandoned on the road "and the balance were run off by Indians on two occasions."

At Fort Vancouver, May 15, 1856, Capt. James J. Archer☆ wrote to his mother in Baltimore that Mrs. Capt. Henry D. Wallen was giving a party that night "in compliment to Maj. Rains' family who are shortly to go to Humboldt where they have no more parties and society. Miss Stella Rains, a gay young lady of 17, seems to regard the proposal pretty much as she would that of being buried alive." Exile to Fort Humboldt on Humboldt Bay, northern California, lasted into 1860, when the major was commissioned, June 5, lieutenant colonel, Fifth Infantry, and assigned to Fort Vancouver. While on leave of absence, he resigned, July 31, 1861, to serve the South.

North Carolinian Rains, born June 4, 1803, thirteenth in his West Point class of 1827, had 24 years with the Seventh Infantry, fought in the Seminole wars and War with Mexico. In the 1840 Florida campaign he was severely wounded and breveted major for gallant and meritorious conduct. As major in the Fourth Infantry, he first was stationed at Fort Vancouver in 1853 and at Fort Dalles, 1853-55.

When fighting the Seminoles he experimented with booby-traps, and in 1862 won notoriety with his ingenious percussion fuse "land torpedoes," planted in a road to delay Federal pursuit from Yorktown. As land torpedoes or mines were considered improper devices by some of his superiors, Rains presently was transferred to river defense, where the use of torpedoes was held "admissable." In August, 1864, the Confederate brigadier used his torpedoes with devasting effect at City Point, Virginia, blowing up two ammunition barges and a new warehouse, inflicting casualties and causing the Union a four million dollar loss. Handiness with explosives was also a specialty of West Point brother Gen. George Washington Rains, who built and managed a most efficient powder mill at Augusta, Georgia, operating throughout the war.

In 1877-80 Gabriel James Rains once more served Uncle Sam —as a clerk in the Quartermaster Department, Charleston, South Carolina.

Col. George Wright commanded the Northern District of the Department of the Pacific, 1856-58, selected the site of Fort Simcoe, and led the campaigns against the Indians of eastern Washington. Later he directed the Department of the Pacific, and after the Civil War the then brevet brigadier general was appointed to command the new Department of the Columbia with headquarters at Fort Vancouver. He was a commander with whom subordinates were generally on good terms. (U.S. Signal Corps photo, National Archives.)

Campaigning with Wright

TO Col. George Wright☆ fell the task of bringing the hostile interior tribes to terms, with or without fighting.

Wright, with three years of service on the Pacific Coast, and a veteran of the Seminole and Mexican wars, had as his command the reactivated or new Ninth Infantry. On his staff were Lt. Col. Silas Casey, Maj. (Brevet Lt. Col.) Edward Jevnor Steptoe☆ and Maj. Robert S. Garnett.☆ It had been planned to send the Ninth to the Pacific Coast by the overland route, to impress the Indians on the headwaters of the Missouri and tributaries of the Columbia. But on receipt of an urgent request for more troops from General Wool, in November, 1855, following Haller's defeat, the War Department decided to dispatch the regiment from Fortress Monroe by way of the Isthmus.

Regimental headquarters was established in April at Monroe with Casey in charge pending Wright's arrival from California. Half of the officers were regulars, most of them newly promoted, and the others were newly commissioned civilians, many with little military experience. Company officers opened recruiting rendezvous in Maine, Connecticut, New York, New Jersey, Pennsylvania, Maryland, Virginia, Ohio, Tennessee. Companies A, F, G were organized in May, B, H and I in June, D and K in August, E in September, C in November.

The Ninth and the new Tenth were uniformed as other infantry regiments, with exception of knapsack straps and waist belts, which were like those of the French light infantry *(chasseurs-a-pied)* and bugles were supplied instead of drums.

The regiment—27 officers, 736 rank and file, and two medical officers—sailed December 15 on the U.S. Mail SS *St. Louis,*

The 1858 "new regulation hat" of the U.S.Army. Made by Warnock & Co. of New York, "for General P. F. Smith, Chief of the Army of Utah," *Frank Leslie's Illustrated Newspaper* (April 24, 1858) thought it "very handsome."

in its wake a wrangle over the use of baggage space. As reported by Col. Joseph K.F. Mansfield,☆ inspector general, the steamship company had filled the hold with its own stores for the SS *Oregon* at Panama, contrary to an understanding that "the entire ship, less the space necessary for the crew and stores for the passage to Aspinwall" was to be at the disposal of the Quartermaster Department. The company said that the washerwomen's tubs, mostly leaky, took up more room than all the soldier equipment. Nothing came of the argument.

Datelined "Steamship *St. Louis,* Near Aspinwall, New Granada, December 23, 1855," a memorial was addressed to the Hon. Jefferson Davis, secretary of war, "for some changes or modification in the present uniform cap of the infantry," signed by 24 officers of the Ninth. The names of Colonel Wright, Lieutenant Colonel Casey and Brevet Colonel Steptoe led the list. "In the light infantry drill, even with the assistance of the chin strap, it has been found impossible to keep the cap properly on the head, and from the nature of the material of which it is made, it soon becomes shapeless and unfitted for parade purposes," said the memorialists. "Very few changes can be for the worse." They asked for "the present cavalry hat with some slight alterations"—the body of the hat "to be less conical and more pliant,'' the gold cord to be replaced by ''the band now worn by us,'' the material for commissioned officers to be fur and for enlisted men felt. They suggested ''the same number of feathers as now worn by the calvalry'' but with ''green as the color, as light blue is never permanent.'' The black felt calvary hat, right brim turned up, soon would succeed the French type shako and be worn throughout the Army until the Civil War. Some of the credit could be claimed by officers of the Ninth.

Another bit of business handled at sea was examination of the newly appointed officers to determine their fitness, as there had not been time before sailing. Wright had questioned that some were suitable. The board, in two sessions, decided that all were competent.

Arriving at Aspinwall December 24 at daylight, the regiment boarded the cars at 8:30 a.m. for Panama City, a four-hour trip on the lately completed, 48-mile railroad built by William H. Aspinwall and associates. At sunset Wright embarked the entire command, barged to the *Oregon* and *Golden Age.* With Headquarters, regimental band and Companies A, B, E, F, I, K, the *Oregon* steamed from Panama Bay on December 26 and arrived at San Francisco on January 12, sailed thence the sixteenth and anchored at Fort Vancouver on January 21, 1856. Lieutenant Colonel Casey and the remaining four companies on the *Golden Age* arrived at San Francisco January 15, transferred to the SS *Republic,* sailed the seventeenth and arrived at Fort Vancouver on January 22. With Companies D and H, Casey sailed January 27 for Fort Steilacoom, took station the thirtieth and command of the post and the District of Puget Sound.

The last night aboard the *Oregon* the ladies and gentlemen ''danced on the deck by the light of the moon,'' Capt. James J. Archer penned home. On shore next day he discovered: ''Fort Vancouver is no post at all. It is only a military station, constructed of log houses for officers quarters at the head of the slope about 150 feet above the river and a quarter of a mile distant from it. It has quarters for 300 to 400 men.''

Arrival of the Ninth brought regular Army strength in Washington and Oregon to about 2,000. Of the 33 companies in the Department of the Pacific, 27 were in the two territories, including nine companies 700 strong finishing the Rogue River War in southern Oregon.

Gen. John E. Wool, commander of the Department of the Pacific, 1854-57 (when he was 71), contended in the public print about the Indian war in the Pacific Northwest, even after his departure for the East.

When the Ninth left Monroe, Major Garnett was on special duty as judge advocate of a general court martial at Fort Washita, Indian Territory (in present-day Oklahoma). On February 5, 1856, he left New York with 392 recruits for the Pacific—299 men and seven music boys for the Third Artillery, 83 men and three music boys for the Fourth Infantry—and five commissioned officers, four laundresses and four officers' servants. Minus a man washed overboard in the Atlantic, the detachment landed at San Francisco on March 1.

In company with General Wool, bound for Fort Vancouver, Garnett sailed on the sixth with 42 recruits for H Company, Third Artillery, and 26 for E and F, Fourth Infantry; the latter debarked at Crescent City. Picking up the Ninth's B and K at Vancouver, he continued on the steamer *Columbia* to Puget Sound, joining Casey at Steilacoom.

Eighteen-fifty-five had closed gloomily for the settlers along Puget Sound, where Indian forays forced the people to keep close to their hastily erected blockhouses and friendly Indians brought timely warnings. Lieutenant William A. Slaughter was shot dead one December night while conversing with scouting companions in an abandoned White River Valley cabin.

In the new year came a turn for the better. On January 26 the crew of the sloop *Decatur* in Seattle's harbor took positions ashore and repulsed an all-day attack on the settlement. Regular troops and volunteers won several sharp engagements, and Kanasket, one of the ablest and most vindictive chiefs, was ambushed as he stole on a soldier camp and slain. By mid-March the war west of the Cascades was virtually over, and on May 19 Colonel Casey at Fort Steilacoom could report it officially at an end.

In the meantime, Wright was preparing for his expedition to the interior, to establish posts in the Walla Walla and Yakima valleys. Wool, who had felt that the whole war was unnecessary and attributable to mistakes of civil policy, believed that a display of force would overawe the Indians. He had intended to establish a post in the Walla Walla before winter closed down, not because he considered it "in any respect necessary for the defense or protection of the inhabitants of Oregon or Washington Territory," but to prevent Governor Curry's militia from taking possession and waging war against the Indians there. In his opinion, the citizen-soldiers were animated chiefly by eagerness to acquire Indian horses and cattle, and the territorial authorities by desire "to promote their own ambitious schemes" and to advance the fortunes of "pecuniary speculators" at the expense of the federal treasury.

Governors Curry and Stevens were highly critical of Wool for his attitude on the employment of territorial forces. They complained that he had refused to cooperate with the civil governments and that he was unqualified to conduct a war against Indians. In denouncing the general to Secretary of War Jefferson Davis, Stevens cited that Wool had not sent troops to his help when it seemed that he, Stevens, would have to fight his way through hostile tribes in returning from the Blackfoot council. In communications to the adjutant general and Davis, Wool blistered the governors as "would-be military chieftains" and called Stevens an "imbecile."

General Wool's first instructions to Colonel Wright cautioned him to "beware the whites in your rear from whom you have as much to apprehend as the Indians in your front." By "whites in your rear" Wool meant, of course, the two territorial governors, whom, he said, did not intend to let the Regular troops win the war. He enjoined: "I would remark that we have no authority to call for volunteers, to employ them or furnish them with supplies. Therefore the less you have to do with them, unless in extreme cases which I do not anticipate, the better it will be for the service. Many of them as well as most Oregonians are for exterminating the Indians and accordingly do not discriminate between friends and foes. The course thus far pursued by Gov. Curry and the Volunteers has only tended to increase our Indian enemies whilst it has subjected the regular service to greater inconvenience or expense. This by wasting the resources of Oregon and Washington without accomplishing the least good."

Wool's controversy with the governors has been laid to Stevens' chiding of the general before a social group of officers and other gentlemen in a San Francisco hotel where Stevens and family were resting en route to Olympia in 1854. As related by Hazard Stevens in the biography of his father, the talk turned to the battle of Buena Vista, "and General Wool loudly claimed for himself all the credit for that battle, disparaging in an offensive manner General Taylor and the part he took in it." Thereupon, says Hazard Stevens, the governor, "whose strong sense of justice was outraged by the boastful and unfair tirade, spoke up and said: 'General Wool, we all know the brilliant part you bore in the battle, but we all know and history will record that General Taylor fought and won the battle of Buena Vista.' Wool, though visibly offended, made no reply to this rebuke, but it rankled and caused a bitter animosity, which subsequently found vent in hostile action and speech." The incident, Hazard wrote, "materially affected subsequent events, as the governor believed."

In support of his objection to volunteer or irregular operations in the territories, Wool had plenty of evidence, in military and other reports, of raids by civilians on Oregon and California Indians, leading to reprisals and summoning of troops. He also could recall that in the Mexican War some of the volunteer outfits were hard lots bent on massacre and pillage.

Wool found on inspection that most of the soldiers were without good shoes and proper clothing, owing to constant service, and that almost all the animals had been rendered unfit, principally in the Haller and Rains campaigns. Too, he said, Curry's requisitions to fit out his expeditions, had practically exhausted the military resources of Oregon Territory, making it imperative to order wagons, mules and forage from California. Before the shipments could arrive, the Columbia was frozen over, cutting communications between Fort Vancouver and The Dalles and also San Francisco for three weeks.

While the regulars were thus immobilized in garrison, Curry's troops moved into the Walla Walla region and became embroiled with the Indians, whose chief, Peupeumoxmox, appeared under a flag of truce, was detained as a hostage and killed during the fighting.

Wright maintained headquarters at Fort Vancouver until March 8 when he started his expedition for Fort Dalles by boat and the Cascades portage. Uniform coats and "flower pot" hats were stored at Fort Vancouver, and officers and men were rigged in blue flannel blouses and slouched felt hats. Sidewheel steamers crammed with troops and towing flatboats loaded with mules, horses, equipment and supplies churned at three to five miles an hour the 44 miles from Vancouver to the Lower Cascades landing. By ox-wagon and wooden tramway, the impedi-

View above from Middle Blockhouse, Cascades of the Columbia, in 1867. On facing page blockhouse itself is visible, on what was later known as Sheridan's Point (eventually washed away). (C. E. Watkins photos, OHS Collections.)

menta were hauled to the upper landing of the five-mile portage, where the steamers *Mary* and *Wasco* provided the power for the remaining 41 miles to The Dalles. The alternate and slower way was by trail from Vancouver, following the north bank of the Columbia to the Cascades, there crossing the river and then by a circuitous and rugged route to The Dalles.

Wright was camped at Five Mile Creek east of The Dalles on March 26, while en route to the Walla Walla Valley, when Yakimas and Klickitats made simultaneous early morning attacks on the portage settlements at the Upper, Middle and Lower Cascades. Escaping from the upper landing, the *Mary* carried the alarm to The Dalles, and the *Wasco* on the other side of the river got up steam and followed. The settlers at the Lower Cascades managed to flee in boats, and a friendly Indian sped down the river in a canoe to Fort Vancouver, literally causing, in Capt. James J. Archer's words, a stampede. As the alarm spread, settlers from miles around flocked to the fort—a collection of log quarters.

The Middle Blockhouse, Cascades. (Watkins photo, 1867. OHS Collections.)

Capt. James J. Archer, Co. I, Ninth Infantry, at Fort Simcoe, here in uniform of brigadier general in Confederate Army. (Signal Corps photo, National Archives.)

"The stampede," Archer related, "pervaded even the garrison. Nearly all the ladies, encouraged by certain old fogies of officers, ran off one night to the stockade of the Hudson's Bay Company. One family went to Portland and another to San Francisco. What is called Fort Vancouver presented the remarkable spectacle of families of settlers fleeing to the fort and families of officers flying from the fort for protection."

With 278 men loaded on the *Mary* and *Wasco* and a bateau of horses for a dragoon detachment, Wright hurried down the river to the Cascades, and Sheridan, with a detachment of dragoons from Vancouver, went up on the *Belle.* Between the two commands, the upper and middle settlements were relieved and the hostiles scattered into the hills. "Little Phil" almost was not spared for his country's service in the Civil War. A bullet grazed the bridge of his nose and killed a soldier near him.

Archer and his friend and fellow Marylander, Capt. Charles S. Winder of Company E (who would die a Confederate brigadier at Cedar Mountain) were in the action, as was Louis Scholl's good friend, Brevet Colonel Steptoe, who led Colonel Wright's advance. Writing, March 30, from the Cascades to his mother, Captain Archer gave a succinct account of the relief of the Cascades: "We returned," he said, "with about 278 men, arriving before sunrise on the 28th, Friday. The Indians were taken completely by surprise. They fired a few shots as we landed and then took cover in the woods and continued to fire until my company and Winders deployed forward at skirmish and drove them off. Col. Steptoe then led our two companies to the Lower Cascades. They (the Indians) were so busy watching Lt. Sheridan who with 40 men from the garrison at Vancouver was working his way up the opposite side of the river that they would not have seen us until we passed between them and the mountain had not Sheridan's men cheered us and not knowing that the Indians were near, some of our men answered.

"This gave them a lesson and they took to the woods and opened a spotted fire from behind trees till we dashed in after them and drove them off as we had done at the Upper Landing. Only one of our men was killed in this day's work. He belonged to Winder's company and was with the men in the woods when he was shot."

In some accounts, a bugle call was credited with alarming the Indians.

The assaults took the lives of 14 civilians, one a woman and three soldiers of the blockhouse detail. Twelve persons recovered from wounds. Wright estimated that "12 or 13" Indians were killed.

Ten of a locally domiciled band of Cascade Indians captured by Sheridan confessed to aiding the hostiles and were tried by a military commission convened by Wright. Nine were hung from a tree and one was sent in irons to Fort Vancouver. Wright said he should have hung the whole bunch because they had been fully aware of the hostiles' intentions and had mingled with them during the fighting.

Lamented sequel to the affair at the Cascades was the slaying of the family of Chief Spencer, Chinook interpreter with Colonel Wright. Spencer's wife, father, a small boy, a niece and two youths, on their way from Fort Dalles to Vancouver, were followed down the portage road by six armed men, seen by Col. Joseph L. Meek, Oregon militia. He told Sheridan at Camp Lower Cascades, who started a search. The family was found garroted. Sheridan reported to Wright the names of the suspects as given by Meek, advising, "They are all at the Cascades at present." None were called to account. Sheridan *(Personal Memoirs,* 1888) said he had looked upon "many cruel scenes in connection with Indian warfare on the Plains since that day, but the effect of this dastardly and revolting crime has never been effaced from my memory."

The interruption altered the plans for Wright's pacification campaign. Wool directed him to march through the Yakimas' territory first, forcing them to abandon it or sue for peace. While Wright was readjusting his sights, five companies of Oregon Mounted Volunteers under Col. Thomas R. Cornelius, probing Yakima country for Indians and livestock, suffered a grievous loss. Captain A. J. Hembree, veteran of the Rains-Nesmith campaign and a distinguished resident of Yamhill County, was fatally wounded leading a scouting party, April 10, up a hill in the region of lower Satus Creek. His body was recovered in a sharp engagement and the expedition retired with it to The Dalles.

Taking Haller's route of 1855, Wright started north from The Dalles on April 28, with instructions to establish a post near the *See-Lah* (Selah) fishery on the Yakima River and another near the site of the Ahtanum mission. The column passed within two miles of Mool-Mool and by the Indian trail to the Naches River, swollen by the spring run-off, impassable to the infantry but presenting no obstacle to the Indians, who swam their horses back and forth.

Waiting for the river to subside, Wright threw up a fieldwork of earth and gabions (large wickerworks of willows filled with dirt) "of dimensions sufficient to contain a company or two and all our stores," he said, which would enable him to move without the encumbrance of a large pack train. This "basket fort," as it was called later by the settlers, was about nine miles above the mouth of the Naches.

From Indians who came and went, he obtained more or less reliable news regarding the whereabouts of the war chiefs and their attendants. "They seem to think, and say," he reported on May 30, "that they had strong and good reason for the murders they committed, both of the miners and Indian agent [Bolon]; the outrages of the former [alleged molestation of Indian women] and the injudicious and intemperate threats of the latter, if true, as they say, I doubt not, maddened the Indians to murder them."

As of that date, he also reported that Colonel Steptoe had joined him with four companies (three of the Ninth and Haller's of the Fourth) and that Steptoe's pack train was returning at once to The Dalles to bring up more supplies. Exclusive of detachments with pack trains, Wright now had about 500 men at the Naches.

Among the newly arrived officers were Archer and his first lieutenant, George W. Carr,☆ of Company I. Daily, after lunch, they would ride around the country. Telling of one such jaunt down the Naches, Archer said in a letter to his mother: "At the point where the river breaks through its barrier into the great plain over which it hastens to join the Yakima stands a high block of columnar basalt, receding at the base so as to form a shallow cave, where protected from the rain and wind, we found a large number of Indian paintings on the rocks, crudely representing, as I suppose, the painter's idea of their deities." That seems first mention of Painted Rocks, pioneer period landmark and mercantile signboard, whereon few primitive markings remain, in a state roadside park.

Wright was visited by several deputations of Indians—a group from the upper branches of the *Na-chess* (Naches), another that had been living at the Ahtanum mission at the commencement of the war and had fled northward to avoid the conflict, and representatives of smaller bands living near the British possessions. But he principally wanted to receive assurances from the powerful head men of the Yakimas. Wright has encouraged on June 9 when Owhi, Kamiakin and "Te-vi-as" (Teias) encamped across the river "and sent the most friendly messages, declaring that they would fight no more, and that they were all of one mind for peace." Presently Owhi and Teias crossed to his camp. Kamiakin warily remained on the other side.

"Owhi," Wright wrote, "related the whole history of the Walla Walla treaty and concluded by saying that the war commenced from that moment; that the treaty was the cause of all the deaths by fighting since that time." And, he added, "Owhi is a very intelligent man. He speaks with great energy, is well acquainted with his subject, and his words carry conviction of truth to his hearers."

The colonel told his callers that, while he pitied the Indians, they were children in his hands and must submit in order to live happily. Otherwise, he said, the consequences to them would be disastrous. They left, with professions of delight, promising to return in five days to return captured or stolen goods and to comply with whatever demands Wright should make. However, they vanished from the country.

On June 13, Wright was joined by Major Garnett with companies B and K of the Ninth Infantry from Fort Steilacoom. Garnett had left on May 28, proceeding to Cowlitz Landing (near the present Toledo, Washington) for transportation up the Columbia.

Bridging of the swift Naches River proved a laborious undertaking. After a trestle-like structure was thrown across the main stream, it was discovered that 600 yards of undergrowth had to be cut through and four or five smaller bridges made. The task was completed on the evening of June 17 and the next morning at sunrise Wright crossed with eight companies—one of dragoons, one of artillery, two of the Fourth Infantry and four of the Ninth—450 rank and file, and encamped that night on the

Drawings of Kamiakin (left) and Owhi, made by Gustavus Sohon, "A private soldier of the 4th infantry, an intelligent and well-educated German," as Hazard Stevens described him. Sohon was at the Stevens Indian councils, 1855. (*Life of Isaac Ingalls Stevens,* vol. 2.)

Wenas. Steptoe was left with three companies to occupy the earthwork, dubbed "Fort Na-chess," which, Wright explained, "is an important spot as a depot and within easy marches of the fisheries."

In a June 20 communication to department headquarters the commander said: "My men are much in want of some articles of clothing, especially shoes, stockings and overalls; I pray that the quartermasters may be able to keep a supply on hand. Shoes, particularly those pegged, last but a few days marching over sharp rocks."

On the third of July, Wright broke camp on the upper Yakima River "near Snoqualmie Pass," and forded the stream and marched five miles and went into camp. The command marched at sunrise on the fourth and followed an unnamed tributary of the Yakima, crossing and recrossing it repeatedly and making 12 miles that day.

"Resuming our march early on the fifth," the colonel reported, "we began to experience some of the difficulties which our

Indian guides had enumerated. The mountains are very high; the trail frequently obstructed by masses of fallen trees, which had to be removed by a pioneer party. Again the trail runs along the sides of a mountain, with barely enough room for a single animal, and, occasionally, the stones and gravel yielding to the pressure, a mule with its pack would roll down the precipice. After marching 12 miles we encamped in the mountains. Marching at daylight on the morning of the sixth, for the distance of five miles, the trail was far worse than that of the preceding day. However, we soon struck a stream and, following its bed and crossing it frequently, at last ascended a high mountain which overlooks this [the Wenatchee] valley, into which I descended and encamped at 1 p.m.''

There Wright was met by chiefs who had visited him in the Yakima Valley and also by Father Pandosy, and found a large number of Indians and their families fishing. The Indians said they would go wherever he directed but first would like to lay in a supply of salmon. He kept, as hostages, Chief Teias, a brother of Owhi and father-in-law of Kamiakin, and the chief's family. Kamiakin, Wright said, had fled to the Palouse country and Owhi had gone across the Columbia. He sent word to the tribes in those parts that ''they must not harbor these renegade chiefs.''

In his report of July 9, Wright advised Wool: ''I marched from my camp on the Wenatcha [Wenatchee] River at sunrise this morning. Our route along the right bank of the Wenatcha was, at times, almost impracticable, the trail passing over rugged mountains, and but a few inches wide, where a single false step would precipitate man or beast into the roaring cataract, 500 feet below. By working at the trail, and then leading each animal very carefully, I succeeded in crossing over the whole command, with baggage, pack train, and three mountain howitzers, safely; at 3 p.m. encamped on the right bank of the Columbia.

''Previous to marching, I made arrangements for the Indians, with their families and baggage, to follow immediately in rear of our pack train, with a company of infantry and a detachment of dragoons as rear-guard. It was nearly 9 o'clock before the Indians could all get off. They have probably a thousand horses, and extended some five miles; with their women and children, of course, they move slow. It is impossible at this moment to say how many there are in all. I left many to fish, and others will cross over by another trail. They were all willing to come with me now if I said so; but as they desire to remain a short time at the fisheries, I had no objections; my principal object being to carry off the large mass of the Yakima nation and locate them permanently and beyond the possibility of their being operated upon by their former chiefs."

Wright commented that in all his recent operations the aid received from Father Pandosy had contributed essentially to their success. The priest, he said, "had great influence with these Indians, and has exerted himself, both night and day, in bringing matters to their present state."

Reporting next from "Camp on Yakima River, Kittitas Valley, W.T., July 18, 1856," Wright said that he had resumed his march on the morning of the tenth and had reached the Kittitas on the thirteenth. Since leaving Fort Na-chess, he said, the command had marched 180 miles over rugged and unfamiliar country deemed impracticable for military operations.

"I have now," he noted, "about 500 men, women and children at this place, with a much larger number of horses and cattle. These Indians of their own accord brought in and delivered up all the horses and mules in their possession belonging to the government, about 20 in number. Were it advisable, I could assemble a much larger number of Indians at this place, but the difficulty of subsisting them makes it necessary to allow them to occupy separate districts of country where fish and roots can be obtained in abundance. . . . To the people now with me, I am compelled to issue at least 250 pounds of flour daily, to enable them to get along. Still I think it better to do this than to send them far away beyond my immediate control. Other Indians are constantly coming in; this party is the nucleus, the central point around which they will all gather in the fall. I have had interviews with nearly all of the Yakima nation, and they are fully impressed with all the folly of their continuing the war; they have been made to feel the inconvenience of it."

At this time the colonel observed that after examining the country pretty thoroughly he was "somewhat at a loss to fix upon the position of a permanent military post," and asserted: "The whole country should be given to the Indians; they require it; they can not live at any one point for the whole year. The roots, the berries and the fish make up their principal subsistence.'' But he believed that the most favorable site for a post was ''a short distance beyond [north of] the Toponish [Toppenish] where there is good timber for building, grass and water in abundance . . . at the point of intersection of the trails from Fort Dalles and the Kamas [Camas] Prairie.''

Worried callers at his camp in the Kittitas Valley were fugitives from west of the Cascades—Chiefs Leschi, Nelson and Kitsap, with a small party of Nisquallies—all desirous of returning to Puget Sound but fearful of the consequences from the civil authorities.

Leaving Garnett with three companies and 25 dragoons at his camp there, Wright marched on July 21 for the *Ah-ta-mim* (Ahtanum) with a detachment of dragoons, one company of artillery and two of infantry. He had been preceded on the trail by Brevet Maj. Pinckney Lugenbeel, with Company A of the Ninth, with orders to assume command of Fort Dalles. Along with him, the colonel took a party of Deschutes Indians and a party of Klickitats, and their families. The former had his permission to fish on the north side of the Columbia, above The Dalles, and the latter to fish and otherwise obtain subsistence on Toppenish Creek, below the military road crossing. Wright halted for two days at the depot, Fort Na-chess, and on the twenty-fifth was encamped on Ahtanum Creek (which he then wrote as *Atah-nam)* 12 miles from the Yakima River.

In a communication to General Wool, he assured: ''I have seen all the Indians, and they are now living at points which I have designated, either near military stations, or higher up on the streams, to enable them to gain subsistence. They are all at this moment very happy and fully convinced that their true policy is to abstain from war and remain forever our friends. I have also dispelled their fears of Kamiakin, who has oppressed and robbed them for many years, and should he ever return to this country, these Indians will all unite against him.''

Responding to a summons from Wright, a band of 40 Klickitats, headed by their venerable chief, Towatax, also called Nikatani, came from Kamas Lake to a council and related their version of the attack on the Cascades. They said, Wright reported, that Kamiakin, by threats and persuasion, induced 20 Klickitats to join a party of 50 Yakimas for that affair.

From his camp on Toppenish Creek, on August 3, Wright informed Wool: "On the 29th ultimo I marched from the A-tahnum to this place, and since that time I have carefully examined the Simcoe Valley, and I have come to the conclusion that my present position is the most desirable one for station for the winter.

"In front of us is an open plain to the Yakima River; and both up and down that river there is a good trail over a level country—one leading to the Selah and Kittetas, and the other in the direction of the Walla Walla. On the To-pon-ish there are oak and cottonwood, and at distance of four miles west of us there is an abundant supply of the best pine timber accessible with wagons.

"This valley is much warmer in winter than any of those farther north, and the Indians now at the Kittetas, and on the Yakima, Na-chess, etc., will all winter here. This is a central point. The roads from the Dalles, Kamas Lake, and from the north, all unite here, and also from Walla Walla. The Simcoe Valley is extensive, affording grass for our animals and sufficient good land for gardening."

The colonel concluded with the interesting observation: "It is out of the question to confine the Indians in this country to a certain district, unless the government furnish their entire subsistence. The whole country between the Cascade Mountains and the Columbia River should be given to the Indians; it is not necessary to the white people. The Indians can subsist themselves if they have it; the mountains, the plains, and the rivers, each in turn affords them food. In the winter they are compelled to live in the valley, and one strong military post will insure their good behavior."

Following that report, Wright selected Mool-Mool, about three miles west of his camp on the eastward bend of the Toppenish. His attention assertedly was called to the site by Sgt. William H. Kohlhauff,* who chanced on it with a small hunting party. "The pleasant shade of the oak trees and the presence of two immense springs satisfied them that it was a far more suitable location for the post than the site on the *Topnish.*" (J. E. F., editor, *The Washington Farmer,* Christmas Day, 1884.)

On August 8, Wright assigned Garnett, with Companies F and G of the Ninth, to begin the construction of Fort Simcoe, and detailed Capt. Frederick T. Dent,* with Company B of the

Ninth, to make a 67-mile wagon road connecting the posts. Before the first of October, said Wright, "our six mule wagons, with an ordinary load, were enabled to travel over the whole distance." He added: "Usually, for about seven months in the year, wagons can be used, and out of the remaining five, pack animals can, if necessary, be used for three months. I propose, however, to have all supplies for Fort Simcoe reach that station by the last of October."

Under the command of Capt. David A. Russell of the Fourth Infantry, a column composed of Company K of the Fourth, Company K of the Ninth, and Company L of the Third Artillery moved out for the Walla Walla Valley, to be joined there by a supply train escorted by Company E of the First Dragoons, leaving Fort Dalles on August 20 under Steptoe, to establish Fort Walla Walla. Wright proceeded to Fort Dalles and thence to Fort Vancouver. From there he reported on August 24 to Pacific headquarters: "Before leaving the Simcoe Valley, I succeeded in recovering the mountain howitzer abandoned by Maj. Haller. I brought it to Fort Dalles; it was uninjured."

The colonel's recovery of the howitzer resulted from Haller's friendly session with Chief Owhi and son Qualchan, also named Thunder, on occasion of their June visit with other quondam hostiles to the Naches basket fort supply depot. After a conference with Wright, Owhi and Qualchan sat with Haller in his tent and discussed the war and virtues of peace. John McKay and express rider William McBean interpreted. Haller pointed out the futility, for the Indians, of further fighting and complimented Qualchan—that he was "wide awake all night, like a watchdog and could steal horses admirably." Owhi said he had a man who could fetch the howitzer if shown where it was dropped on the trail. Haller gave to Owhi a "paper of tobacco," and to Qualchan, who had battled him so fiercely on the Toppenish, "one of my shirts," he wrote in his journal. Both left "apparently much pleased," while the day's talk indicated to him "that the war is closed."

The Rev. Father Pandosy, who lent his influence in the matter of the howitzer, reported to Haller (in the Kittitas as the expedition was completing its summer tour) that the Indians had found the gun after two days of searching. Haller sent three privates with an Indian to get the piece and to borrow a mule and howitzer pack saddle of Wright at the Toppenish. The colonel, about to break camp and resume his march to Fort Dalles, detailed his own men with packer Alex McKay to handle the job. "I am sorry," Haller commented, "my men were not permitted to recover it, as it was my charge when it was lost, and I was anxious to secure it."*

A September 1, 1856, letter to Colonel Wright from Adjutant W. W. Mackall at Benicia Barracks reads: "Major General Wool directs me to say that he approves of your arrangements with the Yakimas and Klickitats; that it is important you should go to Walla-Walla as soon as possible, and attend to the establishment of the post in that vicinity, as previously directed.

"It is also of the highest importance, says the general, that you, the senior officer (the chief man) should see and talk to all the tribes in that region, in order to ascertain their wants, feelings, and disposition towards the whites. It is indispensable, in order to ascertain the causes that brought the volunteers against those tribes, their conduct towards them during their occupation of the Walla-Walla country, and how the friendly Cayuses have been affected. He wishes you to ascertain what became of the property taken from Fort Walla Walla [the old Hudson's Bay Company post].

"He considers it equally important that you should learn the feelings and dispositions of the Nez Perces towards the whites. . .

"The object of establishing a post in the vicinity of the

*Haller's howitzer evidently was the Model 1841 bronze twelve-pounder, commonly called a pack howitzer, and like the other light mountain artillery in current use. The piece, from muzzle to rear of the base ring, measured 32.91 inches. Its bore was 4.62 inches, length of the bore was 28.16 inches, exclusive of the chamber, and the weight was 220 pounds. The vertical field of fire above the horizontal line was nine degrees; below the line, seven degrees. The gun carriage without wheels weighed 157 pounds, one wheel 60 pounds. Complete with implements, including five-pound handspike, sponge and rammer, the carriage weighed 287 pounds. Appurtenant weights were: thill, 30 pounds; bridle, 3; pack saddle and harness, 47; lashing girth and rope, 3; ammunition chest or carriage maker's tool chest, packed, 117; forge chest, packed, 115; ammunition chest, packed, 112; coal sack filled with charcoal, 25 pounds. (The supplemental Prairie Ammunition Cart, 127 inches long and weighing 802 pounds when packed with ammunition, was found to be too fragile for rough hauls and impractical in the Pacific Northwest campaigns.)

Atahnam Mission was, that the troops might be in communication with Father Pandosy. If the post at Simcoe is so placed as to secure this object, the general does not insist on a winter station at the Mission.

"He hopes the officers, particularly the commanders of these posts, will treat Father Pandosy with kindness, and keep alive in him those dispositions by which we have so much profited in information."

Wright ignored Wool's instructions to proceed "as soon as possible" to Walla Walla country, for what reason, the general later commented to New York headquarters, he was "unable to comprehend." The colonel may have felt there was no urgent need for his presence, since Steptoe was on the ground. His dilatoriness would cause him embarrassment.

To General Wool, Wright wrote on September 20 that Steptoe had selected a position on Mill Creek for a post "five miles below Whitman's old mill-site," that Garnett was "vigorously pushing forward the erection of quarters and storehouses for his command the ensuing winter," and that Haller and his company of the Fourth Infantry would arrive in five days at Vancouver and go by vessel to establish a new post at Port Townsend. He concluded with: "It is respectfully suggested that the post established by Col. Steptoe be called 'Fort Walla-Walla,' and that of Maj. Garnett 'Fort Simcoe'."

Saws and Hammers

THE immediate need was for winter quarters, on which some 80 soldiers and nine civilian "mechanics" were put to work. Pine logs were cut in the mountain gap west of the post, hauled by mules to the site and "squared" by whipsawing. Shingles for the roofs were handrived. A brick kiln was built just beyond the oaks fringing the east side of the parade grounds, to provide material for fire places and chimneys and eventually for the brick nogging in the exterior and partition walls of the officers quarters.

When he later submitted his plan for a permanent post, while in Washington, D.C., on January 8, 1857, Garnett said, "There is no rock that can be used for chimney but the soil makes an indifferent brick which may be made to answer the problem." (The "indifferent brick" proved good enough, both for chimneys and nogging, as attested by its condition a century later.)

By the major's ground plan for the permanent post, the structures formed a quadrangle, with the staff and field officers quarters facing the west side of the slightly sloping 420-foot square parade ground. There were to be five such residences, with the commandant's house flanked by four captains quarters. However, the building of the captain's house at the north end of the row did not get further than foundations and sills.

As for the rest of his design, it was substantially carried out—on the north and south sides of the parade, lieutenants quarters and troop barracks, four of each, and, on the north side, the officers' mess. Behind and parallel to the two rows of junior officers quarters and barracks were the quarters for married enlisted men, servants and laundresses, connected company

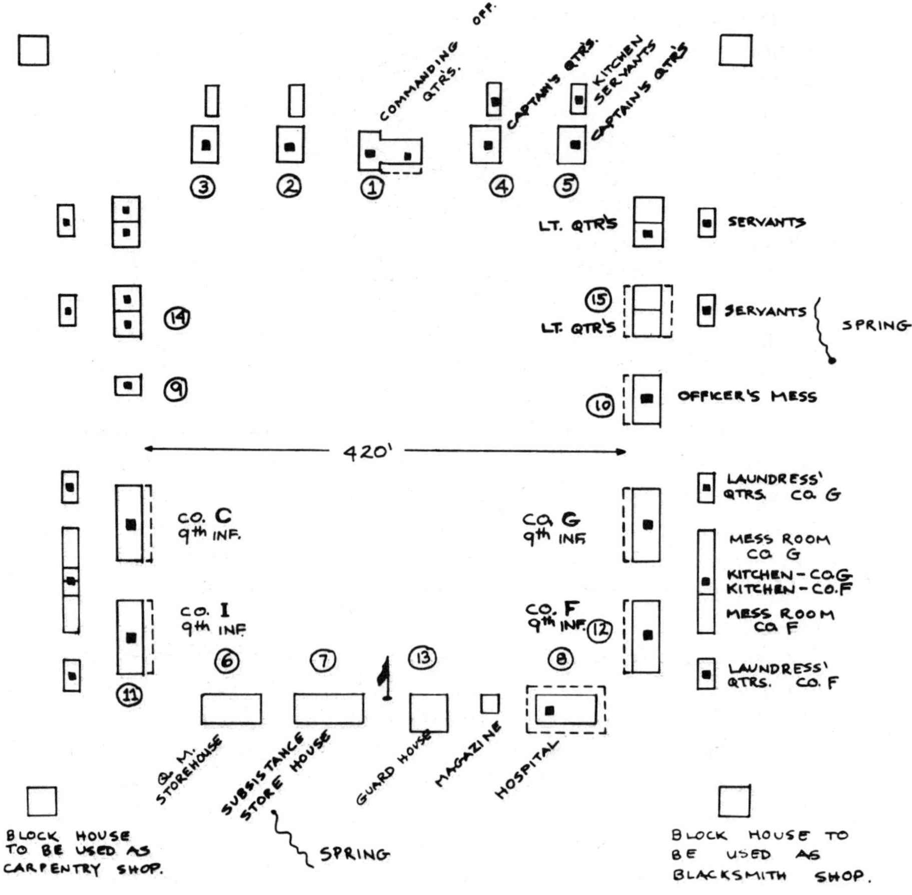

Major Garnett's plan for Fort Simcoe, submitted in January, 1857, when he was in Washington, D.C., to Col. Samuel Cooper, adjutant general of the Army. In accompanying note, Garnett said it was proposed to build those numbered 1 to 10, inclusive, of wooden frame, and all others of hewed pine logs; that those marked 12, 13, 14, 15 were "put up last fall for winter shelter of troops . . ." (National Archives.)

kitchens and mess rooms. On the east side of the quadrangle were, north to south, the hospital, with its dispensary, the guardhouse, subsistence storehouse, and storehouse for equipment and supplies. Between the hospital and guardhouse was the powder magazine. Eight or nine-foot fences of wide boards enclosed the back yards of the senior and junior officers quarters, and also the rear half of the side yards—for protection and privacy. One-story, loopholed, squared pine log blockhouses covered the approaches, that at the southeast corner being designated for regular use as a carpenter shop and that at the northeast corner for use as a blacksmith shop.

At the outset, in August, 1856, Garnett had with him on the job: Joseph B. Brown, assistant surgeon with the rank of captain, Capt. Dickinson Woodruff☆ of Company F, Capt. Francis L. Bowman of Company G, two second lieutenants, Henry Douglass☆ of G and Charles A. Reynolds of F, nine noncommissioned officers and 119 enlisted men, including farmers, musicians, blacksmiths and artificers. Lieutenants John W. Frazer☆ of F and Henry M. Black☆ of G recently had been sent east on recruiting duty.

The command was increased to 218 men in September upon the arrival of companies C and I from the camp that had been maintained through the summer in the Kittitas Valley, near the Indian fishery on the Yakima River. As the authorized strength of an infantry company was 80 men, it may be seen that the garrison was somewhat under the allowable aggregate. Also in September, Garnett's civilian construction crew was increased to 20, drawing wages totalling $2,140 a month.

The post returns carried Garnett's notation that the post was established August 8, 1856, in compliance with General Orders No. 10. "It is situated," said the major, "about 65 miles north of Fort Dalles, O.T., beyond the Simco mts. in the Simco Valley, Yakima country, W.T. It's post office is Dalles of Columbia, O.T."

A sad incident broke the fort building routine—the mad flight and death of 42-year-old Captain Bowman. For several months it had been noted that the captain was having hallucinations which gradually became worse and rendered him unfit for his duties. Finally, on September 4, Major Garnett directed Assistant Surgeon Brown to conduct the captain to The Dalles.

They started at 4 a.m. the next morning with an escort of two men from Company G.

"The captain," wrote Dr. Brown, in his official narration of the affair, "had to be lifted upon his horse as he was suffering from the effects of a severe sprain of his right ankle which he received the night before in pursuing a man whom he fancied to be guilty of riotous conduct toward him. Upon leaving camp he immediately pushed through the oak timber instead of taking the proper trail. I followed him, directing the escort to proceed on in advance upon the trail. After some difficulty we succeeded in effecting a passage through the oaks and soon found the road. The captain took the lead at a fast gallop for a quarter of a mile, when he leaped from his horse, saying that he was tired. After waiting for a few moments he mounted again. He would not receive any assistance in mounting from us as he said that his ankle was well now. He proceeded in this way alternately putting his horse to a gallop and then suddenly dismounting for a few moments, till we reached the *Thopinish.* There he rested some 20 minutes when we proceeded again. After mounting, the captain turned directly back and was returning to camp when I recalled him to the proper direction. He already had diverged from the trail many times but always returned immediately when I called him. He went up the steep hill without dismounting, sometimes urging his horse to a trot. Of course, when I reached the top of the hill he was considerably in advance of me. It was now getting light enough to see the trail quite distinctly and I found that the escort which I had supposed to be in advance had not passed. I accordingly pushed on rapidly and overtook the captain after going about half-a-mile. I endeavored to induce him to wait for the men but without avail, his whole mind being absorbed by the idea of reaching The Dalles without delay."

Brown finally prevailed upon Bowman to take a moderate pace, the latter then explaining he "had arranged everything properly, that he had made a signal to his wife [at The Dalles] who was now expecting him," and that he had received instructions from Heaven to preach the gospel to the Indians.

Reaching a little stream, he dismounted and walked rapidly toward a ravine. Brown caught the horse, dropped the picket rope and loosened the girth so the animal might graze comfortably, and started after the captain. The doctor searched the ravines and jungles until dark, finding only the heel print of an overshoe. The escort belatedly came along. Brown sent the men back to Simcoe with a note to Garnett and rode on to The Dalles.

Parties from both posts and Indian trackers combed the country for a week. On the thirteenth, Indians found a skeleton, identified as the captain's. Wolves had eaten the flesh. Identification was made by fillings in the teeth, some remaining hair and the moustache, Garnett said in a special report. Dr. Brown estimated the date of death as September 10. The remains were taken to Fort Dalles. Officers there and at Simcoe contributed to defraying the expense of sending the captain's wife and daughter, Miss Isadora Bowman, home to Wilkesbarre, Pennsylvania.

Arriving from the camp in the Kittitas Valley on September 13, Captain Archer found Simcoe "a very pretty place, an oak grove on a piece of high land between the Simcoe and the Topinish which unite some miles further down the valley." He commented, "Everybody is busy making bricks, cutting timber, digging foundations and working at building quarters. I don't know what will be the architectural effect when all is finished but the plan is excellent and promises one of the prettiest posts in the country." He doubted that "any more building will be completed this fall than just what is sufficient to afford us all shelter against the cold of winter, viz., two of the company buildings and one house in which all the officers will have to live together."

Taking a sergeant, and accompanied by Captain Dent, Archer departed on September 15 for The Dalles and Fort Vancouver to sort winter clothing for his company. They had a "quite early" breakfast and were across Toppenish Creek before dawn. "We traveled," he wrote, "very slowly all the way in a walk and stopped at a spring about 25 miles from The Dalles at sunset when we built a fire, made some tea and took supper, having first turned our horses to graze, and then laid down on our saddleblankets with feet to the fire and slept until 12 o'clock, got up, breakfasted and traveled on," reaching The Dalles at 8 a.m.

Proceeding down the river from The Dalles on September 19, Captain Archer related that he arrived at Fort Vancouver "just two days late for Miss Lizzie Wright's wedding,'' but had the pleasure of dining with the bride and groom, Lieut. Philip A. Owen, Colonel Wright's adjutant, at the colonel's quarters.

Archer said he was ''invited by everybody at the post to make their house my home during my stay,'' but chose to abide with his friend, Capt. Rufus Ingalls, the quartermaster, who ''took me on a delightful drive (four-in-hand) five miles down the river.'' Visiting ''pretty'' Portland, bustling amid its raw fir stumps, for a session with ''the'' dentist, Archer noted that the people were fashionably dressed and the stores and hotels ''handsome and well furnished.''

Previously, in letters home, Captain Archer had referred to Simcoe as *Sim-Co-E,* but writing under the date of September 30 at The Dalles to his mother, he said, ''I leave here tomorrow evening for Ft. Simcoe.'' That night, the thirtieth, the regiment lost its second officer within a month. Second Lieut. Israel Miller, Co. A, Fort Dalles, drowned in the Columbia River between the Upper Cascades and The Dalles. He presumably fell off the steamer *Mary.*

While peace reigned around Simcoe, trouble was building up in the Walla Walla country, where Lt. Col. Benjamin F. Shaw and his battalion of Washington Volunteers were encamped following a sharp battle on July 17 in the Grande Ronde Valley with Cayuses and Walla Wallas. With a wagon train of goods, Governor Stevens, preceding Colonel Steptoe's column from The Dalles, had joined Shaw for a second council with the Indians. The parley failed and about 450 tribesmen attacked the governor's expedition as it started to return to The Dalles, wounding four men, one mortally. The Indians also attacked Steptoe's camp, which was not far away, but were repulsed by howitzer fire. The volunteers and regulars then withdrew together without further unpleasantness.

Incensed over Stevens' peace effort and the operations of the volunteers, which he deemed interference with the military, General Wool caustically reminded Wright that the latter should have gone in person to the valley previously in accordance with instructions ''too plain to be misunderstood,'' that he had been ordered to ''have nothing to do with volunteers or Gov. Stevens,'' and that he should not have permitted Stevens ''to treat with Indians you have been ordered to subdue.''

Then, with consideration for the feelings of a good officer, Wool wrote: ''But this has been done; and the general earnestly hopes that the annoyance thus given to him may be the greatest cause of regret either he or you may have from the past. Warned by what has occurred, the general trusts you will be on your guard against the whites, and adopt the most prompt and vigorous measures to crush the enemy before they have time to combine for resistance: close the war, and prevent further trouble, by keeping the whites out of the Indian country.''

Wright proceeded to crush the enemy and close the war by marching to the Walla Walla and holding a council with the chiefs. He acceded to their request to ''wash the bloody cloth,'' to bury the hatchet. To Wool he reported he was sure that peace and quiet could be maintained, that the Indians were ''perfectly satisfied'' with the establishment of a military post for their protection. ''I must express,'' he said, ''my decided opposition to the treaty of Walla Walla, and pray it may never be confirmed. All the chiefs in this and the Yakima country whom I have seen are violently opposed to it. Give them back those treaties and no cause for war exists. They proclaim that unfair means were used, whether so or not they will not be contented until after these treaties are restored.''

On October 31, Wright stated, ''I have selected this position on Mill Creek, six miles above its junction with the Walla Walla River, for the post.''

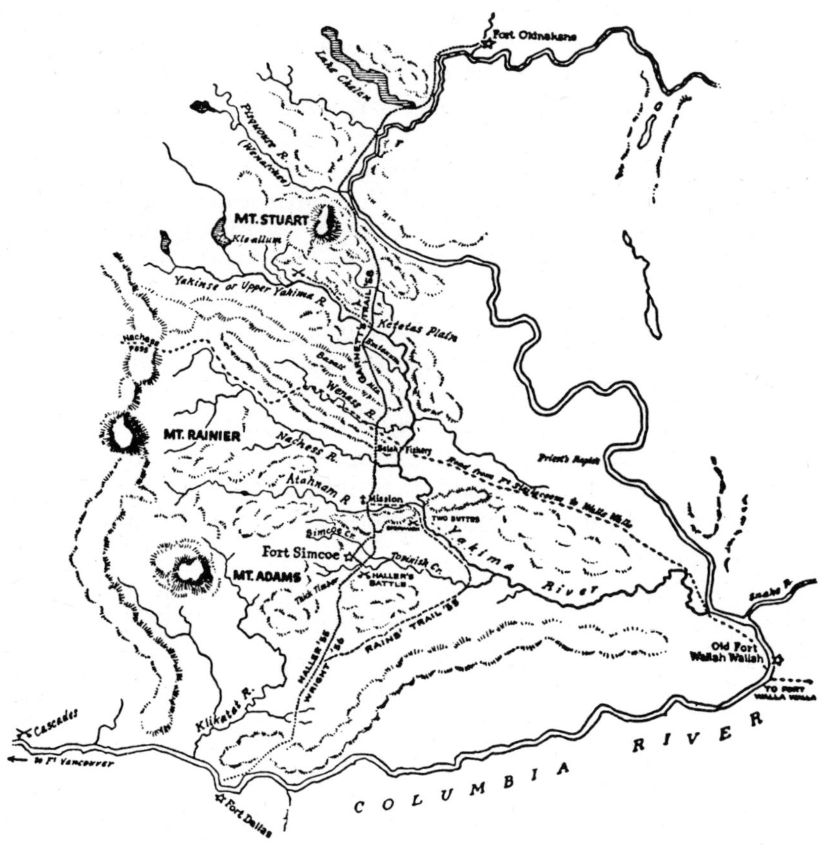

The Region of Operations—based on contemporary Army maps—shows the routes of Haller and Rains in the fall of 1855; Haller's battlefield at Toppenish Creek; Rains' encounter at Two Buttes (Union Gap); Wright's route to the Yakima Valley and beyond in 1856, following the affair at the Cascades; the route of Garnett's northern expedition from Fort Simcoe in 1858, and the Naches Pass-old Fort Walla Walla stretch of the 1853 emigrant road to Fort Steilacoom, subsequently the military and post road between Steilacoom and the Army's Fort Walla Walla.

Shelter from Frostbite

THE autumn was mild, the nicest that Father Pandosy said he had known in his years in the region. The priest, as usual, was shepherding his Indians or, rather, accompanying them, exerting his wholesome influence. He was with them when they moved into the Yakima Valley from the northern fisheries with their packs of cured summer and late-run salmon and set up their mat houses at the Selah fishery below the mouth of Wenas Creek.

At this time of year the Reverend Pandosy ordinarily would be at the mission on the Ahtanum. But the mission was in ashes, thanks to the impetuous arson of the Oregon Volunteers the year before, and the once productive gardens and wheat field were weed grown. The father was reduced, if uncomplainingly, to reliance on the native fare of his charges, nor could he enjoy often with them as of yore a brisket of beef. The thriving herds of cattle accumulated by Kamiakin, Owhi, Teias and others had been scattered and largely lost during the exodus from the valley in '55. Now an Indian was lucky if he chanced upon a half-wild cow to shoot for the larder. So, Father Pandosy took pleasure when opportunity offered to sup with the officers of the Ninth. From him they learned the weather history of the country and that it was not unusual in other years to see ice a foot thick in quiet waters by the first of October.

Easy as was that autumn of 1856, winter was edging down the mountains. On the eighth of October, after a rain, the clouds lifted in the evening to disclose a sifting of snow on the foothills. It vanished under the warm sun of the following day but more showed on the eighteenth and remained for two days. The snow in the hills and occasional cold rains in the valley spurred the builders, especially since Woodruff's company had been ordered to Fort Dalles. The labor of Company F was missed. Woodruff would be gone for a month or more, and they would be longer in getting roofs over their heads. When the fires in front of the tents died down, it quickly got cold inside. Some nights, when the wind was strong off the snowy hills, it was risky to keep the fires going, lest the tents catch. But such was life in the Army.

Major Garnett drove the three remaining companies, C, G and I. Not all the men could be employed in falling and squaring timbers, sawing flooring, splitting shingles, baking bricks, and the civilian laborers, of whom 18 were on the quartermaster's October payroll, were a valued supplement. There were details for camp and guard duties, and a soldier crew was kept busy four miles down the valley cutting wild hay, needed along with the grain hauled from The Dalles for the officers' and couriers' mounts and the work stock. In little excursions around, the officers carried their fowling pieces and brought back pine grouse, sage hen, prairie chicken and jacksnipe for the mess.

All hands were cheered in early November by the arrival of a portable, circular sawmill, which was set up off the southeast corner of the parade ground. Powered by horses or mules harnessed to sweeps, it beat the laborious whipsawing. Mule (or horse) power sawmills were handy rigs and favored by the Army. Small and light, they were easily transportable. That brought over the mountains from Fort Dalles to Simcoe was the same, or similar to, the invention of George Page of Baltimore, to whom a patent was issued on July 16, 1841. It was referred to as the "Patent Saw Mill" or "Page's Patent Saw Mill." In his own description, the inventor called it "my improved portable circular saw-mill." The circular saw was mounted in a sturdy frame, 7½ feet by 4½ feet.

With a 60-day leave of absence, which would be extended, Major Garnett departed on November 19 for the East to get married. Command of the post fell to Captain Archer for two days, until Captain Woodruff and his company plowed in from Fort Dalles in a storm which deposited 14 inches of snow.

Writing to his brother, Robert H. Archer, in Maryland, on December 3, Captain Archer reported it was becoming intensely cold. "I had," he said, "to thaw my ink before I communicated with you and it freezes in my pen as I write, so that I have to hold my pen to the candle to melt it, although there is a big fire just in front of my tent." Continuing the next day, he said, "While I stopped writing a few minutes to warm my fingers last evening the ink again froze in the inkstand and I concluded to lay by my pen until morning." But Thursday (Dec. 4) there was more snow.

"Lieut. Myers [Second Lieut. William Myers☆] who has been absent from the company (I) since October 8, arrived with the expressman. They encountered snow in the mountains two and a half feet deep when it was not drifted. The direct route to The Dalles soon will be impassable but there is another by the Yakima River which we hope to keep our communication with you."

After commenting on the Indian situation along Puget Sound, where the local tribes were quiet but where depredations were being committed by the warlike northern Indians from British Columbia, Captain Archer returned to the affairs of the post. "We are still busily engaged in building and preparing materials. For the last month we have had a saw mill at work with horse (or rather mule) power which has superseded the whipsaw we had been working with. With the exception of one or two citizen carpenters all the labor of building the post is done by the soldiers. Every man of whom is for the purpose on "extra duty" in the Quartermaster Department. Company F (Woodruff's) and G (late Bowman) went into quarters last Sunday. My company and Co. C, Patterson's [Francis E. Patterson] will get in by next Sunday, sure. The officers will get into quarters about a week later. Each officer will have for the winter one room about the size of a tent. When our quarters are all finished, however, which will not be before next fall, we will have ample room. Each captain will have a separate one-story house with a hall and three rooms on the first floor and a back building for kitchen and servants' room. Each lieutenant will have the same except that the quarters of two lieutenants will be under one roof. In the meantime we will be very glad to get the scantiest quarters where we can have shelter."

The officers moved into their quarters on December 14, "not a day too early," Archer commented, as the winter was "now on in earnest" and the snow three to four feet deep. Since the 14-inch fall on November 20, it had snowed three times a week. "Two-thirds of the men of my company," he continued, "were frostbitten before they got in—just one week ago—and nearly all the officers, including myself, are more or less frostbitten." He added that he had found a remedy for frostbite, which had "entirely cured every person here. . . . Stir salt and fresh ashes into boiling water, bathe the feet from 10 to 20 minutes. The bath should be used as hot as the feet can bear it."

The writing of that letter, to his sister "Nannie," was interrupted by the return of two of the men who had started with a pack train for The Dalles on December 7. The train, wallowing in the deep snow of the Simcoes, was forced to turn back on the tenth and make a fresh start by the southern or valley route. "The result," said Archer, "is that about 120 horses, after being completely broken down, have been abandoned in the snow while the packers pushed on toward The Dalles on snowshoes. The two men who returned were much exhausted by hunger and fatigue and badly frostbitten. We have not heard from the rest of the party, neither have I heard of the expressmen who left with our letters on fifth or sixth of December, there being no communication with The Dalles since then. . . . The snow is five feet deep in the valley and must be deeper in the mountains—the Indians have undertaken to carry in our mail on snowshoes and if they succeed will I trust bring back glad tidings from the East where all my treasures are."

In August the captain had assured his mother: "Adams & Co. Express can always be depended on for bringing all the way your letters in the shortest time." The company had an office in Portland. But now only Indians could get through, and the trust in them was not misplaced.

The garrison of the post that December consisted of Companies C, F, G and I of the Ninth, and detachments of Companies C and B, which had been temporarily detained since September 2 on extra duty, to help with the construction. The enlisted personnel totaled 212, of whom nine were in the guardhouse. There were also 15 citizens, mechanics and others, employed at aggregate wages of $1,250 per month.

For reading matter in the long evenings the officers had several official publications—books on military law, medical regulations, infantry tactics, sword exercises, field artillery tactics, mountain artillery tactics, and bayonet exercises. There was, too, a company library of 150 well-selected volumes, specifically noted being essays by Thomas Babington Macaulay and William H. Prescott's "new" *History of the Reign of Philip the Second, King of Spain,* the second volume, published in 1855. There were copies of the popular *Blackwood's Magazine* and *The Illustrated London News,* and weeks-old newspapers like the *Washington Star* and *Daily National Intelligencer.*

The volume on infantry tactics could have lent to animated discussion, as Gen. Winfield Scott, Headquarters of the Army, New York, had a low opinion of the proposed "pet system" of Secretary of War Davis. General Scott called the secretary's "no system at all . . . on account of innumerable blunders and discrepancies." Major Garnett, who had been professor on infantry tactics at the Military Academy, and who was esteemed as "an accomplished tactician" by General Scott, had contributed an exhaustive study on the topic.

Two days after a quiet Christmas the garrison was stirred up by a message brought by an Indian from Father Pandosy, then abiding at the friendly camp at the Selah fishery—below where Wenas Creek enters the Yakima. The priest had word that Chiefs Skloom, Kamiakin and Showawai had crossed the Columbia with a large party of Walla Wallas, Palouses, Spokanes and Nez Perces, and were advancing to attack the post.

While not doubting the genuineness of the father's alarm, the officers believed he had been deceived. They rightly guessed that the information given to him was designed to hold all the troops at the post while the hostiles scooped up 50 head of cattle and 20 horses which had been taken 25 miles down the valley to graze by four herders and a guard of six soldiers. There was only enough forage at the fort for a few horses and a dozen mules used in hauling timbers, and snow three to four feet deep covered the dead grass for miles around.

Woodruff immediately dispatched a rescue party of 20 men on mule-drawn sleds but it arrived too late. With 14 warriors, Skloom had captured cattle and horses and the chief herder, Frederick White. The livestock, left some distance from the guard camp, had been run off the evening before. White had been waylaid when he went out in the morning to look for the animals.

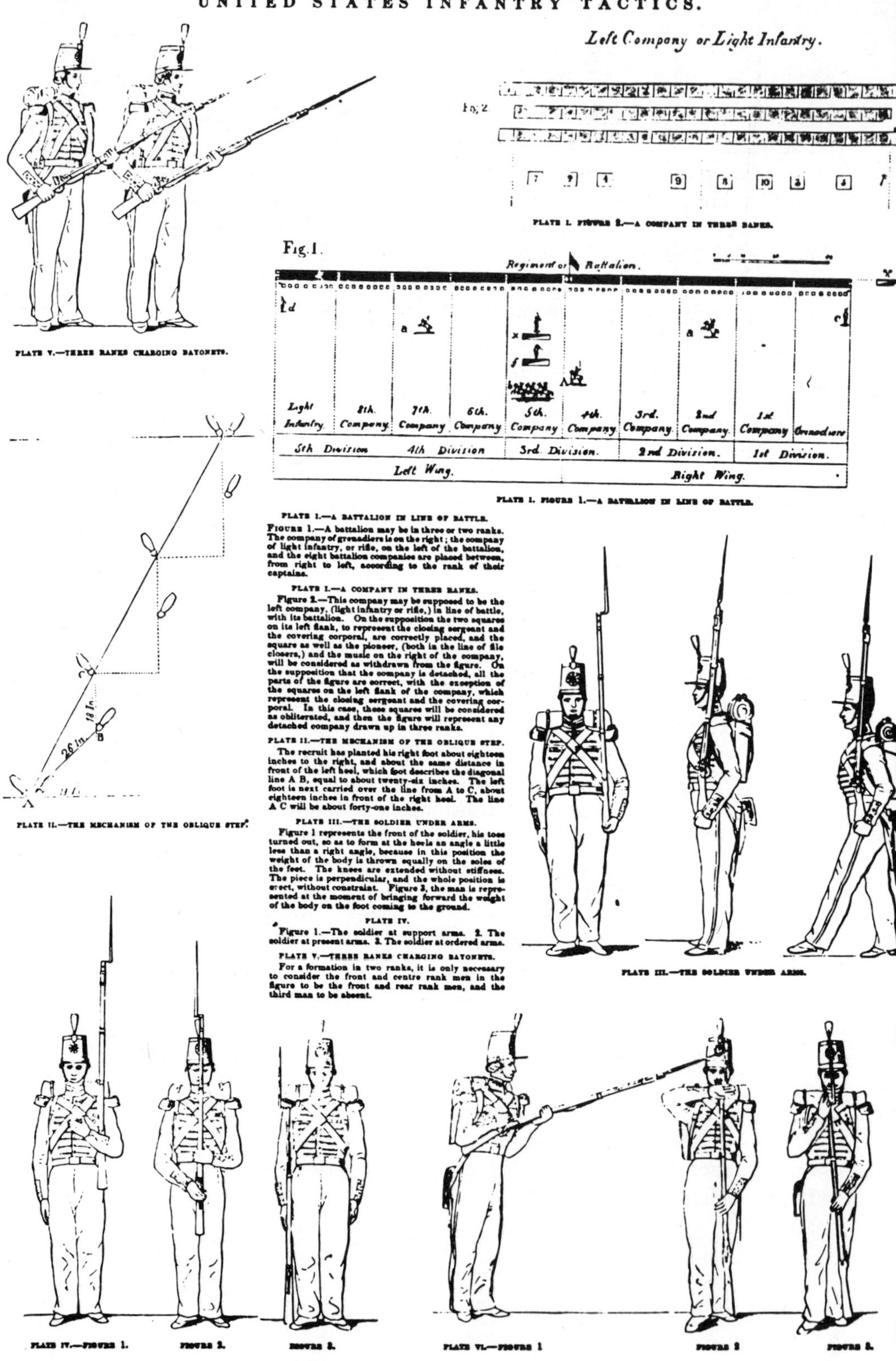
UNITED STATES INFANTRY TACTICS.

Left Company or Light Infantry.

Fig. 2.

PLATE I. FIGURE 2.—A COMPANY IN THREE RANKS.

Fig. 1.

Regiment or Battalion.

Light Infantry | 8th. Company | 7th. Company | 6th. Company | 5th. Company | 4th. Company | 3rd. Company | 2nd Company | 1st Company | Grenadiers

5th Division | 4th Division | 3rd. Division. | 2nd Division. | 1st Division.

Left Wing. | Right Wing.

PLATE I. FIGURE 1.—A BATTALION IN LINE OF BATTLE.

PLATE V.—THREE RANKS CHARGING BAYONETS.

PLATE II.—THE MECHANISM OF THE OBLIQUE STEP.

PLATE I.—A BATTALION IN LINE OF BATTLE.

FIGURE 1.—A battalion may be in three or two ranks. The company of grenadiers is on the right; the company of light infantry, or rifle, on the left of the battalion, and the eight battalion companies are placed between, from right to left, according to the rank of their captains.

PLATE I.—A COMPANY IN THREE RANKS.

Figure 2.—This company may be supposed to be the left company, (light infantry or rifle,) in line of battle, with its battalion. On the supposition the two squares on its left flank, to represent the closing sergeant and the covering corporal, are correctly placed, and the square as well as the pioneer, (both in the line of file closers,) and the music on the right of the company, will be considered as withdrawn from the figure. On the supposition that the company is detached, all the parts of the figure are correct, with the exception of the squares on the left flank of the company, which represent the closing sergeant and the covering corporal. In this case, these squares will be considered as obliterated, and then the figure will represent any detached company drawn up in three ranks.

PLATE II.—THE MECHANISM OF THE OBLIQUE STEP.

The recruit has planted his right foot about eighteen inches to the right, and about the same distance in front of the left heel, which foot describes the diagonal line A B, equal to about twenty-six inches. The left foot is next carried over the line from A to C, about eighteen inches in front of the right heel. The line A C will be about forty-one inches.

PLATE III.—THE SOLDIER UNDER ARMS.

Figure 1 represents the front of the soldier, his toes turned out, so as to form at the heels an angle a little less than a right angle, because in this position the weight of the body is thrown equally on the soles of the feet. The knees are extended without stiffness. The piece is perpendicular, and the whole position is erect, without constraint. Figure 3, the man is represented at the moment of bringing forward the weight of the body on the foot coming to the ground.

PLATE IV.

Figure 1.—The soldier at support arms. 2. The soldier at present arms. 3. The soldier at ordered arms.

PLATE V.—THREE RANKS CHARGING BAYONETS.

For a formation in two ranks, it is only necessary to consider the front and centre rank men in the figure to be the front and rear rank men, and the third man to be absent.

PLATE III.—THE SOLDIER UNDER ARMS.

PLATE IV.—FIGURE 1. FIGURE 2. FIGURE 3.

PLATE VI.—FIGURE 1 FIGURE 2 FIGURE 3.

Book tactics were modified in frontier field actions like the Yakima War; but these might have been seen on the Fort Simcoe parade ground.

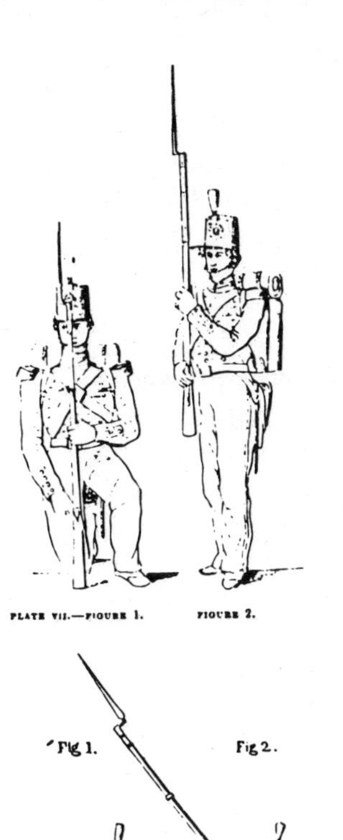

PLATE VII.—FIGURE 1. FIGURE 2.

Fig 1. Fig 2.

PLATE IX.

PLATE VI.

Figure 1.—The position of the soldier having executed the first time (or pause) of loading in four times. 2. The position of the soldier having executed the second time of loading in four times. 3. The position of the soldier having executed the third time of loading in four times.

PLATE VII.

Figure 1.—The front rank men in the position of ready. 2. The centre rank men in the position of ready.

PLATE VIII.

Figure 1.—Front rank men in position of aim. 2. Centre rank men in the position of aim. 3. Rear rank men in the position of aim.

PLATE IX.

Figure 1.—The soldier in position of trail arms. 2. The soldier in position of arm shifted to the right shoulder.

PLATE X.

Figure 1.—Position of the feet of the three ranks, in the fire direct by the squad or company. 2. The position of the feet of the three ranks in the oblique fire to the right by the squad or company. 3. The position of the feet of the three ranks in the oblique fire to the left by the squad or company.

PLATE XI.

Represents a company marching by the right flank, and wheeling by file to the left, and next by file to the right.

Figure 1 represents the company marching to the right flank. The right guide is before the front rank man on the right to conduct him, and the captain is placed on the left of his guide. The file closers are placed two paces from the rear rank, each abreast with his place in the line of battle. 2. Represents the company wheeling by file to the left; the front rank men do not turn too suddenly, they describe a short arc of a small circle, and the centre and rear rank begin to lengthen the step before arriving at the angle formed by the two directions, in order to come up more promptly abreast with their respective file leaders, now on the left. 3. Represents the company wheeling by file to the right. The wheel is made on the same principles as the wheel in figure 2. In each figure the instructor is placed near the point of change of direction, in order to watch over the execution of the movement. 4. Represents a company marching by the right flank, and forming itself on the right by file into line of battle.

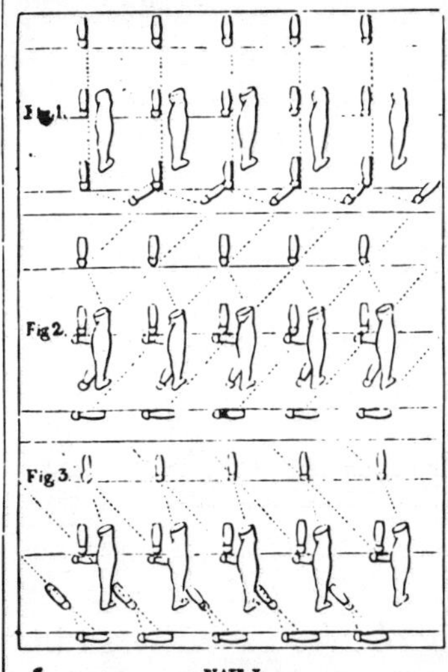

PLATE X.

The head of the company being abreast with the point at which the right is to rest, the movement has commenced; the centre and rear ranks have marked time.

The covering sergeant has turned to the right, and the captain has conformed himself to the movement of this sergeant; the captain has been halted by the instructor at the instant he had arrived on the line of battle, and the covering sergeant has placed himself behind the captain.

The front rank man, on the right, has continued to march straightforward, and after having passed the covering sergeant, he has turned to the right to come up on the line of battle on the left of the captain; the second man of the same rank has continued to march; after having passed the first, he has turned to the right to move up and place himself on the left of the first. The third man has done the same thing in respect to the second, and so on of the others.

As soon as two men of the front rank had placed themselves on the line, the centre rank ceased to mark time, and began to advance. Each man of this rank has placed himself behind his file leader, in conforming himself to what has been prescribed for the front rank, or is in march to do so. The rear rank has next formed in like manner, or is in march for the purpose, having begun to advance on seeing two men of the centre rank established on the line.

Six men of the front rank, four of the centre, and two of the rear, are already established on the line.

The instructor has followed the movement from the right towards the left of the line.

Figure 5 represents a company marching by the right flank, and forming itself by company into line. The covering sergeant has continued to march straight forward; the captain has moved rapidly some paces in front, and has faced to his company to superintend the movement.

The men have advanced the right shoulder, and have taken the quick step in order to reach the line by the shortest lines; the men of the centre and rear ranks have each followed the exact trace of his file leader; the files have arrived, or are arriving on the line successively, and, on arriving, each has taken, or will take the step of the guide.

The company preserves the touch of the elbow towards the right till the captain commands *guide left*, when the last file has arrived on the line.

Fig. 4.

PLATE XI.

ANOTHER BRITISH SHIPMASTER ENFORCING THE FUGITIVE SLAVE LAW.—The *Pensacola Democrat* of the 24th of July, says "The English ship Sarah, bound to Barcelona, which was towed out over the bar on Sunday last by the Cuba, returned day before yesterday and made signs for a pilot outside. After having gone about a hundred miles the captain discovered a negro man, who had secreted himself on board. He was taken charge of by one of our pilots and brought to the city. This we consider very handsome conduct on the part of the captain, especially as he had suffered much annoyance from the desertion of his own crew, while here, from the lack of efficient legal aid in recovering the deserters."

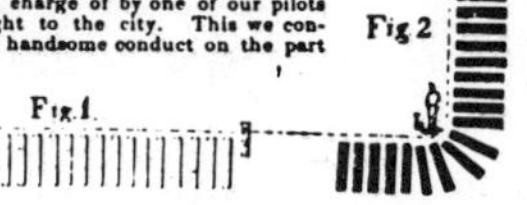

PLATE XI.

THE INFLUENCE OF THE LONDON TIMES.—It may not be generally known, says a cotemporary, that the leader of the "Times" is telegraphed every morning to all the principal towns of England; then written out in large letters and affixed to a bulletin board, and is placed in the public Exchange. At Glasgow, Liverpool, Manchester, and other towns of less commercial importance, crowds of merchants and others may be seen early in the day reading this article! As it thus, in effect, does the thinking for the mass of the middle classes of Great Britain, its influence with them must be very great. It is difficult, in fact, to understand its extent and power, which no class, we presume, and not even the Government itself, fails to acknowledge.

PLATE XI.

EJECTING A RAILROAD PASSENGER.—Henry McEwen, a resident of Brooklyn, was disorderly in one of the Second Avenue Railroad cars, last week, and refused to pay his fare, when John Haggarty and P. O'Neil, the driver and conductor, ejected him. In being pushed out, McEwen's foot caught under the wheel, and was crushed. He was sent to the Hospital. The driver and conductor were arrested, but subsequently discharged, it appearing that McEwen was the only one to blame.

TO PREVENT HYDROPHOBIA IN DOGS.—An exchange recommends the following: "To prevent dogs becoming mad, take as much African cayenne pepper as will make a pill about the size of a large pea. Give this in raw meat once or twice a week during the warm months, and you will have no mad dogs."

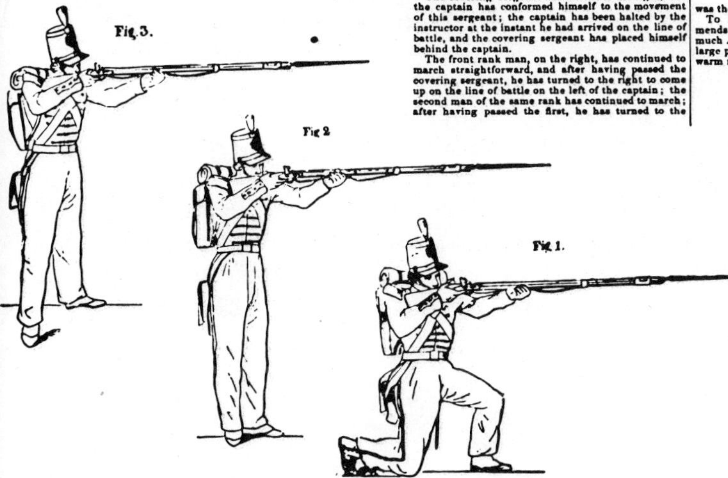

PLATE VIII.

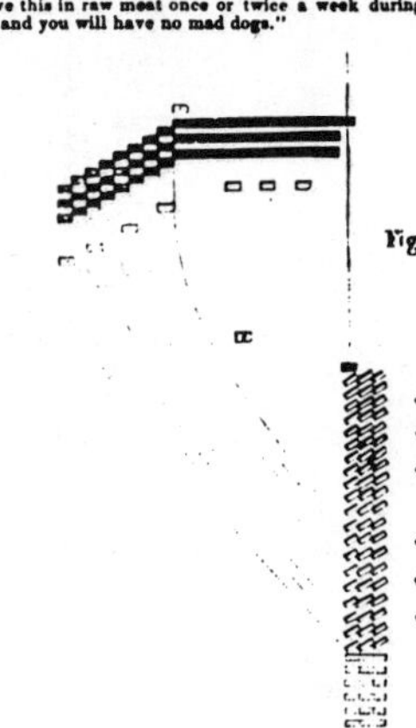

PLATE XI.

From *Frank Leslie's Illustrated Newspaper* (New York), August 23, 1856.

From White presently came several letters, written in his native German, describing his capture and plight and the attitude of the Indians, and containing messages from his captors. The missives, delivered by Indians, were translated by one Casco. The translations, forwarded to Colonel Wright at Fort Dalles, are in the National Archives. The morning White was made prisoner, the Indians took him across the Yakima River, built a fire, ate a little, and proceeded to White Bluffs on the Columbia, reached on the third day. From there White sent his first letter, dated December 31. The young warriors, he said, had wanted to go into the guard tents and kill all the whites and take the Indian herders prisoner but were dissuaded by Skloom, whom he called Skilloom. White said in the beginning he was not sure of his life "for a single hour."

Through White, Skloom made overtures for peace, but he was advised by Captain Woodruff, in reply of January 1, 1857, that peace was up to Colonel Wright. The captain told Skloom to continue to treat White well "and send him safe to me," whereupon he would tell Wright that "Skilloom, Chief of the Yakimas, is a true man, and has but one heart and one tongue."

Writing on January 12 to Lieut. Jesse K. Allen,☆ White acknowledged receipt of some of the things the officer had sent by Indian messenger. "The overcoat, the blanket, tobacco, paper and half the victuals I did not get," he lamented. "Please send me four pounds of tobacco, soap, fine comb, a razor and some paper . . . But few of the [captured] cattle are alive, eight have been killed and a good many have died. I am living like an Indian. What he eats, I eat. Where he sleeps, I sleep also, but I cannot complain of bad treatment."

Important information received from White during his captivity was a list of the names of the murderers of Agent Bolon, divulged to him in the Indians' accounts of the causes of the war. "They say," he wrote, "six of their young people went to The Dalles to buy fish. They met Mr. Bohlen on the way. One of these Indians had been out hunting and five Indians with their wives met Mr. Bohlen. Their names, Mitchell (Showawash son), Wattashin, Nanginim (an old man)—these two live on the Kabisk—Woppy, Sukei and Stuchen. Three of these six killed Bohlen. The one by the name of Stuchen caught him by the beard and cut his neck with a knife. Woppy held him by the arms and Sukei by the feet. When Skilloom and Showawash heard of this they were very angry, as Skilloom and Bohlen were great friends.'' The names thus became handy for future grim reference.

Woodruff, relaying that intelligence to Wright, said he would consider it ''expedient'' to make those Indians prisoners should they visit the post. He commented ruefully that Mitchele or Michelle (Mosheel) had twice visited the post in the autumn.

For the perpetrators of the Bolon killing, White's capture was indeed an unfortunate occurence. Two of them—Woppy (properly Wah-pi-wah-pi-lah) and Stuchen (Stah-kin) eventually were caught and hung from a Fort Simcoe oak, and Mosheel was fatally shot in attempting to escape. Sukei (Soqiekt) shot and killed himself after the war. Wattashin (Wah-tah-kon) who returned from hunting after the crime was committed, was thrown from a horse and killed 15 years following the war. The old man, Nanginim (Nou-yan-nan), who had remonstrated with the killers, died a natural death.

White was held for two weeks at White Bluffs, given a horse and saddle by Skloom, and released. He apparently continued right along in the employ of the Army, as he was one of Major Garnett's packers in the campaign of 1858.

Through the minor excitement, work went on at the fort. A track was kept beaten up the gap to the lumbering operations, now three miles distant. But construction was slowed on January 9 when the master wheel of the mule-power was ''again broken beyond the possibility of putting it in working condition,'' Woodruff reported, continuing, ''We have therefore been forced to rely for boards entirely on the manual labor which cannot supply enough to keep the citizen mechanics employed. The quartermaster has in consequence discharged three of them.''

Winter in its bleakest aspect was suddenly over on January 19. The weather turned mild overnight—the garrison's first experience with a chinook. Out of the draws and gorges poured snow water, and the ground became mud. On the twentieth, Indians who had taken out the last mail on showshoes returned from Fort Dalles with official dispatches and private mail—eagerly seized news from home.

As soon as travel conditions permitted, Woodruff, on February 1, sent out his post returns and correspondence by regular express, and members of the garrison took the opportunity to include their personal mail. Woodruff informed Wright that he had just issued 6,780 pounds of flour to the bands from "the Selah, Na-chess and Topanish, 615 in all," and said that in the middle of January he had afforded the sanctuary of the post to Indians wintering on Toppenish Creek, on their plea that they feared an attack by Skloom. He also told of a council held that morning with Owhi, son Qualchan, and a son of Teias, who came to talk about peace. The captain was "not convinced of the sincerity of their declarations" and he was nettled by the sauciness of Qualchan, whose language "was not pious." He was provoked, too, by the flounderings of the interpreter, a mixed-blood named Brown, "very deficient in knowledge of English" although he might "answer well enough for an express rider," which employment the officer recommended.

In February the post learned of the promotion of Henry Douglass of Co. F from second to first lieutenant, and the promotion of Lieut. Henry M. Black (absent on recruiting duty since he was detached May 30 at Camp Na-chess to go East) to captain.

Word came that General Wool was transfered to the Eastern Department in accordance with his request of December 4. Therein he stated that it had been nearly three years since his assignment to the Department of the Pacific command, that he had not entirely recovered from the last of several attacks of sickness, and that the department was well organized and the posts judiciously located "with reference to the protection of the white inhabitants and the control of the Indians."

Brevet Lt. Gen. Winfield Scott and Secretary of War Jefferson Davis endorsed the request, approved January 8, 1857, by President Franklin Pierce, who wrote: "Let General Wool be relieved." It had been just about a year since the Oregon territorial legislature, January 20, 1856, adopted a memorial to the President praying recall of the venerable officer from the Pacific command. The people, the memorial said, "had lost all confidence in the willingness" of General Wool "to assist and defend them in their present Indian difficulties."

The Simcoe post returns for March noted the first death in the command since that of Captain Bowman—"Thomas Foley, private, 9th infy. C, died, March 20, '57."

Hangman's Oak, east of Simcoe parade ground, where two of Indian agent Bolon's murderers were executed and several other Indians hung. Tree was pointed out by late George Olney, in this 1938 picture. Simcoe's white oaks are the Garry oak (Quercus garryana), largest in the Pacific Coast region, commonly attaining a height of 50 or 60 feet and 18 to 30 inches in diameter. The wood is hard, fine-grained, tough and durable. The acorns are sweet and still harvested by some of the Indians. (H. D. Guie Collection.)

Veranda of the Fort Simcoe CO's quarters, before restoration, with porch of captain's quarters beyond. Note narrow floor boards under rocker. (H. D. Guie Collection.)

Ladies, Birds, and Flowers

FOR the annals it was a happy circumstance when Capt. Anthony Heger,* assistant surgeon, Army Medical Department, received his Special Orders No. 136 at Benicia Barracks, California, on November 15, 1856, to proceed to Simcoe. Captain Heger drew one of the two known sketches of the post; Mrs. Heger's correspondence contributed to its story; William Simcoe Heger—the first white child born at Fort Simcoe—added to the record.

From the Middle Cascades of the Columbia, on November 27, Annie Whitney Heger wrote to her sister, Miss Kate Whitney, at Pottsville, Pennsylvania, about their trip that far. They had left San Francisco at 10 a.m., November 18, aboard the Steamer *Columbia,* shortly became seasick for the five-day voyage and did not emerge from their stateroom until the ship was ready to dock at Portland. The next morning they took the little sidewheeler *Fashion* up the river, but the elements seemed still to be against them. The wind grew so violent that the captain hauled to overnight, and it was the following evening before they were landed at the Lower Cascades, on the Oregon shore. (The *Fashion,* on its downstream run, struck a reef and sank. It was raised, repaired, and continued to ply the Columbia until 1861.)

Their traversing of the portage, accompanied by a soldier, was a slow and wearisome leg of the rather arduous journey. Behind a four-mule team, "with trunks and all," they jolted over a road "much worse than any at home" for about a mile, rowed in a small skiff about two miles on a lake-like branch of the river, and then walked a mile "over the most lonely road

Annie M. Whitney Heger, (above), wife of Capt. Anthony Heger and mother of Fort Simcoe's first white child, William Simcoe Heger.

At right, Brig. Gen. Anthony Heger, who was captain and assistant surgeon at Fort Simcoe. (Photos courtesy General Heger's granddaughter, Mrs. Charles Donald Shane, H. D. Guie Collection.)

through nothing but dense woods, not a habitation in sight, with such feelings,'' said Mrs. Heger, ''as I cannot describe.''

They came to a house, the headquarters of Joseph S. Ruckel and Harrison Olmstead, operators of the portage route and owners of the *Fashion* and also the *Wasco,* which made the run between the Upper Cascades and The Dalles. Surprisingly, this Mr. Ruckel was an old acquaintance of Mrs. Heger, whose brother had married his cousin. The last that Mrs. Heger had heard of the now ''very stout and healthy looking but quite as handsome as ever'' co-proprietor of the transportation system he was living in California.

The next day the doctor roamed the woods and shot three grouse. That night three inches of snow fell. On November 28, with the long winter closing in, the travelers boarded the *Wasco,* Mrs. Heger mightily pleased with Mrs. Ruckel's generous gifts—a box of yeast powders and a pound of precious butter that had cost a dollar in Portland. Fort Dalles, crowded waypoint of unfinished quarters and workmen everywhere, was as far as they could get. For the Hegers, it turned out, Fort Simcoe was still three months away.

Colonel Wright, December 4, mentioned in a dispatch to headquarters at Benicia that Heger ''leaves today for Fort Simcoe.'' He reported on the sixteenth that the captain ''went out with the train but couldn't cross the mountains and returned to Fort Dalles; he will try again to reach his station with the express.'' A copy of the captain's orders arrived at Simcoe by Indian snowshoe courier on the third but none at the post looked for the new doctor until the worst of winter was over and the road again open.

Writing, March 7, 1857, to William Gibson in Germantown, Pennsylvania, Louis Scholl☆ said that Dr. Heger, his ''countryman'' and ''fine fellow,'' just left that day for Simcoe. Mrs. Heger, as Scholl delicately expressed it, was among the Ninth's ''married ladies'' looking ''very charming and promising.'' She would remain, he said, at Fort Dalles, ''all summer,'' but Mrs. Heger actually did not stay so long.

In the same letter Scholl informed Gibson that the Fort Dalles colonel's quarters at last was finished—Scholl had lived in the kitchen all winter—that bakehouses, officers quarters and a stable for 50 horses were nearly finished and that Dr. Brown's

Louis Scholl, who drew the plans for Fort Dalles buildings, and also for Forts Simcoe, Walla Walla and Colville. Photo made at The Dalles in 1856. (Courtesy Louis Scholl, Jr., H. D. Guie Collection.)

Above, "Dr. Brown's house" (Surgeon's Quarters, Fort Dalles), with construction scaffolding. Below, Colonel Wright's quarters, where Scholl lived in kitchen during winter of 1856-57 (the colonel and his family were at Fort Vancouver). (1857 photos, Ft. Dalles Collection, OHS.)

house would be ready for him by Christmas. Also complete, he said, were six smaller buildings for noncommissioned officers and cooks.

Captain Heger's overdue appearance at Simcoe excited expectation of other early additions to post society. Major Garnett would be bringing his bride. Proud of his lately sewn captain's stripes, Mrs. Black would be accompanying her husband. Second Lieut. Charles A. Reynolds of Company F would have his February bride. Whether the wife of Second Lieut. William Myers of I Company would join the distaff of the garrison was doubted. Mrs. Myers had tasted frontier existence, lastly at Fort Dalles in 1855, and, her husband indicated, was content to remain home in Cincinnati.

March was mild, and before the end of it Captain Archer put in a vegetable garden—an enjoyable diversion—for his company. He wondered if the mice in the stockyard might not discover his plantings. But it was not the mice he had to fear—in due course the crickets moved in and set to nought the enterprise. By mid-April in that soft spring the oak grove was almost in full leaf and wild flowers of every hue decorated the country around. Going horseback, said Archer, was "like riding through an immense flower garden."

With springtime in his heart, the naturally amiable and now apologetic Skloom rode in with a following to return the horses he had stolen. He also brought a few lean beeves that had not succumbed to the winter or the appetites of his people. Luckily, he had prevailed on his warriors the night of the raid not to shoot down the soldiers in their illumined tent, so there was no blood on his hands. The restitution, accepted by Captain Woodruff, enabled Skloom and his band to go about their root gathering and salmon taking without the distraction of an avenging military.

Elsewhere the signs were propitious for peace or at least a state of no hostilities. From Fort Walla Walla came word that Chief Kamiakin was expected to appear with an offer of surrender—an optimistic report, although he caused no trouble that season. But the Nez Perces were reliably friendly, and the Cayuses, Umatillas, Walla Wallas, Spokanes and Palouses were said to be of a mind that Colonel Wright would restore all their country to them, and thus not disposed to renew the fighting.

Lieutenant Reynolds and the attractive Mrs. Reynolds, who quickly became a great favorite, arrived on April 21, accompanied by Second Lieut. James B.S. Alexander. ☆ April saw, too, the employment, for the first time, of a house painter at the high wage of $4.00 a day, which also was the prevailing rate for carpenters, whose number that month was increased from a half-dozen to 20. The new carpenters were a welcome addition. Through the winter and spring, real and feigned illness had cut the soldier work forces. An "unusual number" of the enlisted men had been sick with "rheumatic complaints and the want of antiscorbutics." Many had been shirking hard labor "under the plea of illness." The maladies of the latter could be cured, it was observed, if the Quartermaster Department would provide the funds necessary to pay the soldiers for their nonmilitary tasks.

With a detachment of 121 recruits for the four companies, Major Garnett and Captain Black marched into the post on May 17, swelling the garrison to 348 men. For Mrs. Garnett and Mrs. Black, it was a haven after their long voyaging by sea and land. They all had sailed from New York on April 5 to Aspinwall, crossed the Isthmus by train, boarded ship again and reached San Francisco on April 30. Of that bustling city, familar to the major from previous visits, they had but a glimpse. On May 5, 1857, they debarked at Fort Vancouver, remained only overnight and proceeded up the Columbia to Fort Dalles.

There, while the recruits drilled and regained their land legs, and preparations were made for the 65-mile march north, the ladies had a nine-day respite. From the rising, handsome new quarters of the Ninth Infantry they could look up and down the broad and fabled River of the West. By the distant progress of speck-like horsemen, pack strings and wagon trains they could trace the route soon to be taken over the seemingly smooth, transiently green hills on the Columbia's far side, toward the expanse of the Klickitat Valley and the forested flanks and crests of the Simcoes where snow yet lingered. With garrison wives, and gallantly escorted, they could stroll or ride down the piney slope to the waterside town and there watch the fussy landings of the paddlewheelers, laden with military supplies and merchandise, and the tooting departures of the little craft for the fast downriver run to the Upper Cascades.

One of the steamers brought Captain Archer from Portland,

where he had hoped to find the traveling dentist, only to learn that the busy man had left for Puget Sound. Meeting the arrivals from the East, the captain was "especially pleased" with Mrs. Garnett. "She," he promptly wrote to his mother, "is pretty, intelligent and perfectly ladylike. She was a Miss Nelson of New York. I think the major's rough manners are much softened and improved by the feminine influence."

Indeed, the feminine influence exercised at Fort Simcoe by the major's lady, by Annie Whitney Heger, Mrs. Black and Mrs. Reynolds was most agreeable. Living took on long-missed niceties, with the paying of calls, jolly evenings of games and song, and the dining at tables conventionally set and agleam with treasured pieces of silver flatware in the mellow radiance of candles and oil and camphine lamps.

Sweeter now, certainly, to the masculine ears was the music of the flitting songsters of the oak grove—the meadowlarks, grosbeaks, redbreasted robins and the golden orioles whose basket-like nests hung high in the trees—and less dolorous the notes of the turtle doves. Perhaps almost musical were the rough voices of the crows and magpies.

There were walks and picnics, visits to the Indian huts by Mool-Mool Creek and over on the Toppenish, horseback jaunts that sent the coyotes loping through the sage and put prairie chickens to wing, and rides to vantage points or up the west canyon a mile to the quarry where the stones for the building foundations were cut and shaped, and beyond to the timber workings in the redolent yellow pines.

The last of May came all too soon, for then Woodruff had to depart with his Company F to serve as an escort for the American Northwest Boundary Commission, assigned to begin the survey of the line with the British Possessions. That meant also the departure of the popular Mrs. Reynolds. Her lieutenant had sought unsuccessfully to exchange the detached service duty with a fellow officer, so Mrs. Reynolds properly decided to accompany him to the damp and forested northwestern corner of the territory, cheerfully undaunted by the prospect of camping out.

Baptized on a Billiard Table

A BIG June event was the birth of fittingly-named William Simcoe Heger. Mr. Heger's "Recollections," written about 1936, provide the following account: "Fort Simcoe, June 17, 1857. At this frontier fort in Washington Territory I was born on the above date, baptized on a billiard table, my godfather being McFeeley of the subsistence corps whom I did not see again until I was 21 years old in Washington, D.C., when he was Maj. Gen. McFeeley and I told him he had given me but little care.

"The way I happened to be baptized on a billiard table was this. The houses under roof in this little stockade fort were scarce and this particular room was used as the officers club during the week and on Sunday the billiard table was covered and church services held there. As a gift the officers sent to Portland and bought me a silver cup and with a pen knife cut my name 'Willie' on it. This cup, somewhat battered, is still in my possession. I have gathered that the first white baby born in their midst was a great object of interest to the Indians, who would flatten their noses against the window panes to watch my mother bathe me, much to my mother's discomfort. My first nurse was an Indian girl and my playthings as I grew up to them were home made.

"At the time of my birth my father made a sketch of Fort Simcoe on a sheet of brown paper [see p. 84] and later on made some photographic copies of it showing the quarters where I was born.

"From Fort Simcoe my father was ordered to Fort Vancouver on the Columbia River near Portland. . . . While at Vancouver

William Simcoe Heger, first white child born at Fort Simcoe, June 17, 1857, to Capt. and Mrs. Anthony Heger. (Courtesy his daughter, Mrs. Charles D. Shane.) Lower right is "Willie's" silver cup, gift from officers of post. (H. D. Guie Collection.)

Right, Katherine Doherty (Mrs. Zenas Arizona Moody), first white girl born at Fort Simcoe, Sept. 6, 1857, to Pvt. and Mrs. Jeremiah A. Doherty. (Courtesy her son, Z. F. Moody.) Below, old soldier Jeremiah A. Doherty of the Ninth Infantry, at The Dalles. (H. D. Guie Collection.)

my father received orders to go to Pt. Lookout, Maryland, to take charge of Hammond Hospital. This was during the Civil War and I must have been six or seven years old. We came to San Francisco and were to take the Steamer *Golden Gate.* We were delayed in reaching San Francisco and the *Golden Gate* sailed without us or these memoirs never would have been written, for from the date of her sailing no word was ever heard of her.''

Godfather ''McFeeley'' (Robert Macfeely) Fourth Infantry quartermaster, came up from Fort Vancouver for the christening. Pennsylvania appointee, thirty-first in West Point's class of 1850, his first frontier station was Fort Dalles, 1852-53. He commanded an escort with Governor Stevens' Pacific Railroad Survey exploration, the northern route, 1853-54, and the latter year, out of Fort Dalles, scouted after Indian marauders on the Oregon Trail. First lieutenant (February 3, 1855-May 11, 1861), he was with Major Rains' Yakima expedition of 1855, in the Rogue River, Oregon, hostilities, during March-June, 1856, and until in 1860 continued as quartermaster at Fort Vancouver. Through the Civil War he participated in several campaigns and rose in rank in the subsistence department. He was breveted colonel in 1865 for ''faithful and meritorious services during the Rebellion.'' On April 14, 1875, he was named commissary general of subsistence, receiving promotion to brigadier general. He retired July 1, 1890, died February 21, 1901.

Mrs. Heger was a busy mother that first summer, as she pointed out in a letter of September 13 to her sister-in-law, Miss Theresa Heger, in Pottsville. Asking to be excused for her ''seeming neglect in not writing before this to inform you of the arrival of Willie Simcoe Heger,'' she explained. ''My time is employed all day. Wc havc so much difficulty with servants, half the time we are entirely without anyone, and now of course the whole care and nursing of the boy comes upon me. I have no one to hand him to but the Dr. who is indeed always ready to help me. Were it not for him I should despair of ever getting along. We are entirely dependent upon our own exertions in this wild country. Servants who come here with families are not satisfied, become disgusted and soon leave. What can we expect else, no inducements to offer them. It is only persons who are compelled to live here who stay any time.

"We are not yet in our permanent quarters, the Post not being completed. We are obliged like others to wait patiently until our house is finished. Since we number 3 in family our rooms appear quite too little. . . . You were kind enough in one letter to give me the latest fashion in dressmaking. It benefits me but little as no opportunity offers to procure the necessary articles to make things fashionable, notwithstanding it's always pleasant to be posted up in the world. We should be lost indeed to everything new and fashionable were it not for hearing through letters. My little boy has interrupted me twice while writing, something new as he generally sleeps all morning. He is the best child ever born, never crys, [*sic*] a stranger would not know he was in the house, and exceedingly sweet and pretty, so we think at all events. My great desire now is to bring him home for inspection among his many Aunts and Grandmother. The Dr. has gone out gunning, game is quite plenty, he always brings home a half dozen or so of grouse and ofttimes ducks. They are acceptable as the meat is not so good."

After the death of his mother in 1864, William Simcoe Heger lived alternately with his Aunt Theresa in Philadelphia and relatives in Vienna, visiting his father as opportunity offered. Altogether he made 12 crossings of the Atlantic, received much of his schooling abroad and graduated in electrical engineering from Stevens Institute, New York. In 1882 he married Miss Alice Lea Ferris, of Wilmington, Delaware. There were four children.*

Ireland's calamitous potato blight and ensuing famine, which forced one of the great migrations in modern history, sent tens of thousands of Erin's sons and daughters to America and gave to Fort Simcoe its first white infant girl. At the post on September 6, 1857, Katherine Doherty was born to Sgt. and Mrs. Jeremiah Doherty, G Company, both once of County Donegal. A proud day it was for the garrison's wearers of the green.

*Mr. Heger removed with his family to San Francisco in 1889 and was early associated there with the General Electric Company. For many years he was Pacific Coast manager for the Westinghouse Company. From 1905 to 1910 he was assistant to the president of the Allis-Chalmers Company in Milwaukee, Wisconsin. He then returned to the coast and was with the Busch-Sulzer Diesel Engine Company until he retired in 1916 to his home in Belvedere on the shore of San Francisco Bay. He died on October 30, 1937. (Mrs. Charles Donald Shane, nee Mary Lea Heger, surviving sister of the late William Simcoe Heger, Jr., provided this biographical material.)

The sergeant and his Esther, the former Miss Nelis, were wed October 15, 1856, in St. Peter's, New York City, by the Rev. Father Downing. The groom was a civilian between enlistments. Six-footer (5-11-¼) Doherty first joined the Army on June 5, 1851, in New York. Age 23, his papers said, complexion ruddy, eyes hazel, hair dark, occupation clerk. Assigned to Company A, Permanent Party, General Service, at a local depot for training and forwarding recruits, he was made corporal, November 15, 1852, and sergeant on August 18, 1854. In June, 1855, when the new Ninth Infantry was being organized, he was transferred to it as a private, and enrolled in F Company. He was appointed sergeant July 1, and first sergeant in January, 1856, on shipment of the regiment to the West Coast. He fought at the Cascades of the Columbia, in the opening of Wright's campaign. Discharged at expiration of service, June 5, 1856, he returned to New York.

Re-enlisting on March 21, 1857, Doherty was put in the Ninth's Company G. A private in Captain Black's detachment of recruits and accompanied by Mrs. Doherty, he arrived at Fort Simcoe in May. On June 1 he had new sergeant's stripes. He tramped north with the Garnett expedition of 1858. Following the evacuation of Simcoe, his stations were Fort Dalles and Fort Vancouver. He completed his enlistment in the Quartermaster Department, San Francisco. Honorably discharged on March 21, 1862, at the Presidio, he rejoined Mrs. Doherty and daughter at The Dalles, where the family residence was established in May, 1859.

Jeremiah Doherty of the Ninth Infantry, born August 11, 1829, died at The Dalles, on April 19, 1909, five days after the passing of Mrs. Doherty. Born December 25, 1833, Esther Doherty died on the fourteenth of that April. Burials were at The Dalles.

On May 15, 1892, Katherine Doherty was married to Zenas Arizona Moody, whose father, Zenas Ferry Moody, 1851 pioneer, a former state legislator and governor, was prominent in Oregon business development. To Mr. and Mrs. Z. A. Moody were born sons Zenas Ferry Moody, Eugene D. Moody and daughter Edith Moody. The line was continued in two grandchildren, sons of Mr. and Mrs. Z. F. Moody. Fort Simcoe's Katherine Doherty Moody died on December 28, 1928, at San Carlos, California.

The Major Wants It Nice

MAJOR Garnett had troubles that summer of 1857. There were no hostile Indians—the bands in his district and elsewhere were professedly friendly—but the Quartermaster Department at San Francisco was displaying a vexing streak of economy. It turned down requisitions for materials and for additional "civilian mechanics." It had failed to ship funds for extra duty pay. Soldiers working alongside civilians receiving $4.00 a day were grumbling and shirking. Many feigned illness at sick call and some took French leave.

Extra duty pay was 50 cents a day. In 1854 the pay of enlisted men in the lowest grade had been increased $4.00 to $11 a month. Soldiers serving in the West were entitled to double pay but the government retained half of the increase until honorable discharges were issued, apparently to discourage desertions. So, 50 cents a day was a substantial increment, worth having to spend at the sutler's store.

The major's problem respecting the use of troops for construction of the post was not particular to Simcoe. It was common along the expanding frontier, as noted by Secretary of War Jefferson Davis in his report of December 1, 1856. "The authorized strength of the army, as now posted," he said, "is 17,894. The actual strength at the date of the consolidation of the returns, July 1, 1856, was 15,562. The number of enlistments made during the 12 months ending September 30, 1856, was 4,440. The number of persons offering to enlist, but who were refused on account of minority and unfitness for service, was 5,594. The number of casualties in the army, by deaths, discharges, and desertions, during the year ending June 30, 1856, was 6,090; of which 3,223 were by desertion."

The secretary continued: "the frequent construction and abandonment of posts, and with such garrisons as we may expect to have with the present or probable size of the army, involves the employment of all the troops for long periods of constant labor, alike injurious to military instruction and the contentment of the soldier. His compensation at such times is far inferior to that of the common laborer on the frontier and the prospect of abandoning the position soon after he had made it comparatively comfortable leaves him without an adequate inducement for the sacrifice he is called on to make. A laborer without pay or promise of improvement in his condition, a soldier without the forms and excitement of military life, it is hardly to be wondered at that this state of things should lead to desertion, which has become so frequent as to be one of the great evils of the service."

Those were Major Garnett's sentiments exactly. Writing on July 28 to Major Mackall, adjutant to Gen. Newman S. Clarke—General Wool's successor as department commander—Garnett repeated a request he had made in May for the ordering of a general court martial. He advised that the "full penalty of the law" be applied speedily for the good of the discipline of the post. The number of prisoners now under charge of the guard," he said, "exceed that of the guard itself and though as many of them I could obtain irons for are heavily ironed they have within a month made three bold and well executed attempts at escape, each of which was near proving successful."

To Lt. Col. Thomas Swords, deputy quartermaster general at San Francisco, Garnett declared that the building of the post by troops was not a "proper or legitimate occupation." Had his requisitions been granted, he said, he could have given his command proper instruction in soldierly duties. "But as it is," he commented, "the best part of another season will have to be occupied in labor, and the command, half soldiers and half mechanics, thus continued in a condition little better than that of a well organized horde of laborers. This result is justly laid at the door of the Quartermaster Department. No military man will contend that troops can be properly disciplined and instructed when they are compelled to handle axes more than arms."

Relating that Captain Ingalls of the Quartermaster Department at Fort Vancouver recently had informed him of a shipment of $5,000 to Fort Walla Walla for extra duty pay, Garnett chided, "In not supplying this post with at least an equal sum you have deprived me of the most efficient means I could have had of [carrying on] the work before me."

Other excerpts from the letter to Colonel Swords further illuminate the major's difficulties, while providing information pertinent to the restoration program. "In regards to the 120 barrels of lime called for by me as necessary for the completion of the post, you decide that 20 are sufficient," he said. "Twenty barrels of lime to build a four company post in latitude 46, 30 N. Mechanics who know how to perform this feat ought to have been sent along with the lime. None such are here. Your reasons are that 120 barrels of lime appear to be a great deal more than should be required for the quarters at your own post where a material, cheap at its place of transportation but exceedingly expensive when it has been transported so great a distance should be sent in the most sparing manner. Are you prepared to say that lime has been used here in any other manner or that the requisition was made with the intention of using it in any other manner than one demanded by the most rigid economy?"

Garnett explained that the lime had been used only in "those parts . . . exposed to the action of fire (fireplaces) and those exposed to the weather and in pointing log quarters," that in all other work only common mortar was used. "And," he continued, "such was the manner in which it was intended to use the 120 barrels called for with the addition only of underpriming, whitewashing, plastering a small portion of the frame quarters (commanding officer's and captains' houses).

"The shortsighted economy of using mortar so much in lime has already manifested itself here and during the coming winter will do so to a much greater extent. One of the chimneys put here last fall, the very last one, is now in such condition that it will have to be pulled down and another put up before the winter. The labor thus thrown away could have brought lime in the first place for three chimneys, to say nothing of the time thus taken up. To be sure, the brick was bad and the weather very cold, but still had the mortar been capable of hardening properly the chimney would not have been so very unfit for use."

Capt. Anthony Heger's sketch of Fort Simcoe, made in June, 1857, on a sheet of brown paper, shows the post near completion; interior finishing in senior officers quarters (far side of parade) and high fencing remained to be done. A fifth house in the row (note ground outline) was projected. (Photo given H. D. Guie in 1954 by Mrs. Charles D. Shane.)

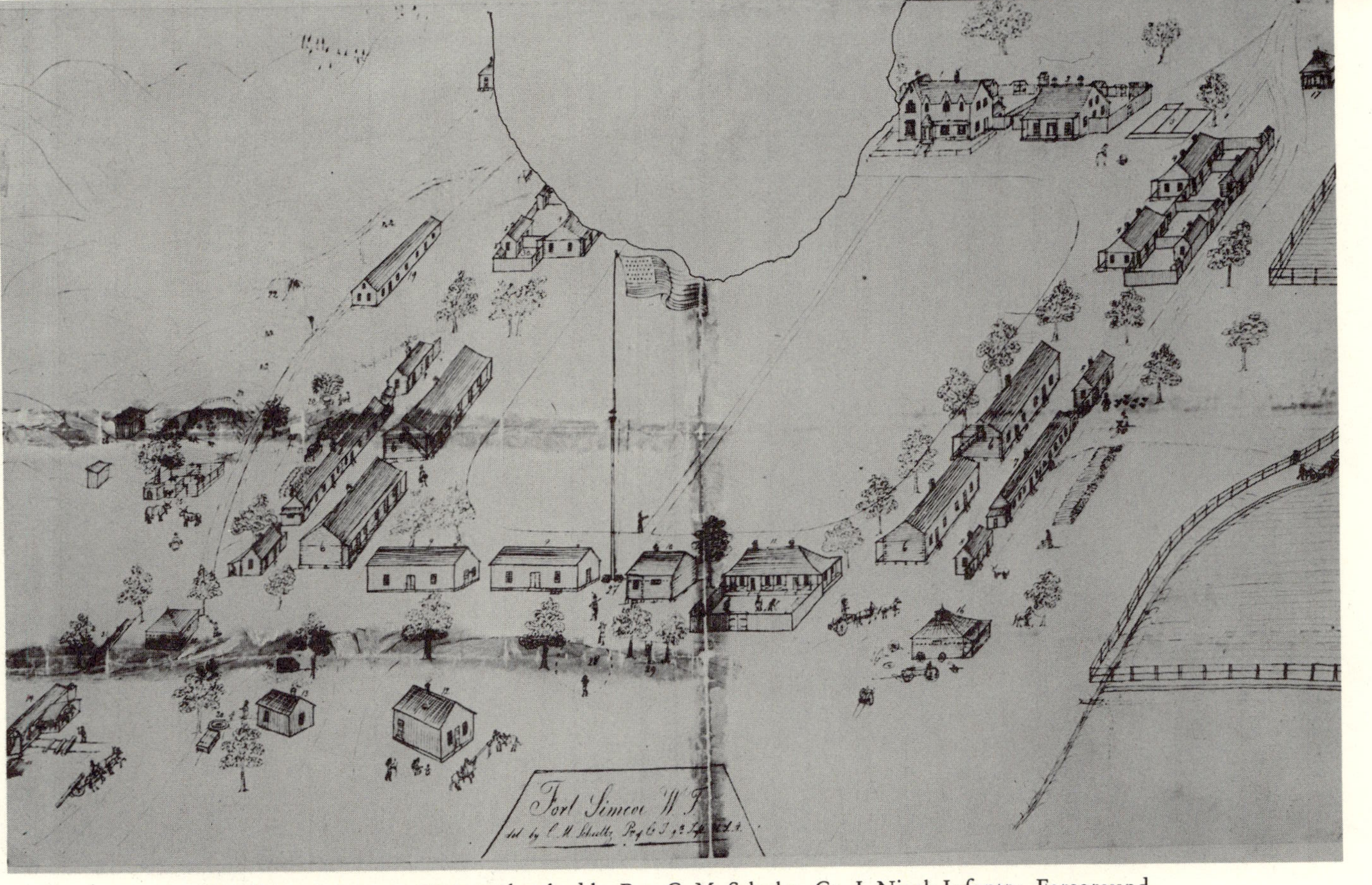

Fort Simcoe, summer 1858, as sketched by Pvt. C. M. Schultz, Co. I, Ninth Infantry. Foreground, far left, log delivery to mule-powered mill; bakery by spring; sutler's store, Indian family, horses at rail, prisoners walking circle. Left of flagpole: commissary store, quartermaster's store. Right of flagpole: guardhouse, hospital. Blockhouse at right used as smithy. Small buildings back of barracks on either side of parade were quarters for laundresses. Upper right, woman and go-cart. Also right, fenced gardens. (Courtesy Ronald Todd, Univ. of Washington Library.)

Views of CO's quarters. Above, restored, with kitchen wing at right. (Louis H. Martin photo.) Below, winter view from rear before restoration; kitchen wing left, bathroom right. (H. D. Guie photo, 1940.)

The major observed that his original instructions to finish the interior of the quarters in wood, readily obtained, because wood was cheaper than plastering, did not take into account the dryness of the climate. "Boards," he said, "warp, shrink and crack to such an extent that you cannot make a permanently tight wall with it. All the flooring and all the board lining and ceiling which I put up in the quarters last fall will have to be taken down this fall, as soon as I can get other buildings up for the accommodation of the command, and replaned and put up tight again. How long to remain so, I cannot tell. And this process will have to be gone through with next fall with these buildings which I complete during the present time. Do you wish me to understand you that these [labors] by mechanics at $4 per day or even extra duty men are cheaper than a finish of plaster which would end the matter at once? And you take no account of the time thus taken from more legitimate and professional occupations of my men."

Among Garnett's requisitions had been a turning lathe, which the deputy quartermaster general had seen fit to deny as unnecessary for the "comfortable or even neat appearance of the legs of bunks." Such reasons, the major asserted, were not controlling considerations. He pointed out that among the enlisted men he had "an excellent turner" who had been sick all winter with scurvy and who was still afflicted when the requisition was made out, but able and wanting to work at his trade of turning.

"My design," Garnett said, "was to get a lathe attached to the saw mill and set this man to work. By winter when the carpenters could only be employed at indoor work and I perhaps would be able to spare a few from other work to make these bunks I should have all the legs ready to put together. But now, in consequence of the action in the return, this time of my carpenters which is mostly precious will have to be taken up in planning and finishing these legs."

The major was pleased that his request for a spare master wheel for his sawmill, which he proposed to obtain at Portland, had met with the colonel's approval. He remarked: "One extra master wheel on hand to prevent loss of time by accident as had frequently occurred before was all I wanted." But he felt it had been poor economy to refuse his request for fire brick because, in Swords' words, it was "entirely too heavy an article to justify its transportation.'' The colonel had said: ''If no substitute can be found near the post, good fire stone, easily cut, can be had as I was informed at The Dalles.''

''No substitute near the post can be found as I thought I told you when you were here, nor can we make one,'' Garnett said. ''As to the stones at The Dalles, I got Capt. [Thomas] Jordan to send me up some during the time my requisition was awaiting action. But the mechanic who quarried them is now here putting them up. He is a very skillful man and tells me it took him three days faithful work to quarry and [get] enough (soft as it is) to make one fireplace. He is employed at $5 per day. Each fireplace thus costs $15 at The Dalles. He tells me it requires 128 fire bricks for one fireplace and that fire brick cost 2½ cents in San Francisco, making $3.20 the cost of a fireplace in S. F. I cannot be made to believe that it would cost $11.80 to send 128 bricks to The Dalles nor even half of it. It would be near $90 per M for transportation. I should like to contract with the government for half that sum. Moreover, the stone would have to be quarried and dressed and this takes time. Your views of economy on this item are not less doubtful to my mind than in previous one. It is a fatal mistake to imagine that the great cost of building in this country is due to the cost of materials. It is not so. The enormous wages which labor brings is the true cause of it. Material or rather lumber is rather cheap in this country than otherwise and so would be the stone if it did not cost so much to prepare it for use.''

With no less sarcasm, Garnett took up the treatment of his request for material for stoves. ''The six sheets of iron (the next item mentioned in your letter) were asked for to build cooking furnaces in the kitchens of the four companies belonging to this post. Three are now here and were here when you were. One is temporarily absent about on the Boundary survey. You direct Captain Ingalls to send 'two sheets of iron of the kind required, being one for each company kitchen.' You seem to think that there are only two companies or company kitchens here. There are four, one for each company. Six sheets were asked for; four to form the entire surface of the furnaces (one for each furnace) and two to be cut up to make doors. The other two ranges I shall have to build of indifferent brick and worse mortar to tumble by next summer and then to be rebuilt. All this may be economical but I fear it will not pass muster under that name, particularly next summer. It is too late now to get stone from The Dalles in anything like sufficient quantity. It will be as much as the train can do (and I fear greatly more) to haul our subsistence and clothing for the winter. Much valuable time has been lost by the slow movement of the train induced by the necessity of stopping at The Dalles to forge shoes.

"Those 20 barrels of lime, or rather 19 of them, have arrived. As also four small sheets of iron which by riveting can be made into two of the size wanted. But it is proper to state that previous to the arrival of the lime I had succeeded in begging some 16 or 17 barrels from Captain Jordan. Those, with the 19 and what Captain Jordan may have left from his own use, may keep the masons at work until it gets too cold to work in mortar, but upon the buildings which will be nearly ready by next spring before wagons can reach us, I shall have to stop work for want of mortar to put up the chimneys."

Noting that no mention had been made of his requisition for white lead, Garnett observed, "The white lead was wanted chiefly to prime and paint the board work in the hope that it would prevent the shrinking and cracking to a sufficient degree to render it unnecessary next year to take them down and refit them. If my hopes were realized, a great expense would have been saved the government. It was at least worth the trouble."

In a letter of July 14, Swords had communicated Clarke's wishes in regard to the completion of the commanding officer's quarters and the erection of additional buildings. "I regret," Garnett remarked, "that the General was unable to make a personal inspection of the post himself [when he visited Fort Vancouver in June]. It must necessarily have been more perfect and satisfactory to him than any report which staff officers or myself could make to him.

"I presume the plan of the commanding officer's quarters originally proposed was the one submitted to the General and hence the misapprehension under which he seems to labor in relation to the principal floor. The plan was somewhat changed by me after my arrival here in the spring in order to cut off or isolate two attic rooms for commanding officers and adjutant officers. As I thought I explained to you when you were here, there are only four apartments on the principal floor which could be deemed assignable for an officer's habitation. As I thought I then told you, the four rooms, my authorized allowance, are more abundant for my new individual wants. The two remaining attic rooms could only have been subscribed to me as providing for the comfort of the occasional military visitors of the post whose duties unhappily bring them to this distant region."

He assured: "The two upper rooms of the commanding officer's quarters, cut off as offices, I propose to finish plastering for these purposes unless the General desires otherwise. The remaining two attic rooms will remain unfinished as he directs." The other buildings, he added, would be put up according to his original plans "or according to plans still more economical if it be satisfactory to the General."

Getting no satisfaction from the deputy quartermaster general at San Francisco in the matters of white paint and a sufficiency of lime, Garnett finally (on November 4) appealed to Secretary of War Davis, addressing his request to Col. Samuel Cooper, adjutant general, at Washington, D. C. Commenting that the department commander had instructed him to use whitewash instead of common paint, the major said: "This material when put upon wood—for I have also been refused a sufficiency of lime for plastering—is known to be unfit for the habitation of persons who desire to preserve those habits of neatness and cleanliness common among the class of people in civil life from whom the officers of our army are supposed to come.

"In making this application I deem it proper to add to it the broad declaration that there is no officer in this department who has used greater personal exertions in his own sphere of action though limited and humble it be; or deserved more earnestly than I do to observe a just economy in the expenditure of all public money instructed to his care; and it affords me a particular gratification to challenge for this statement the closest examination.

"But while I claim for myself the credit I desire it proper to say that I consider it equally my duty to see that the small portion of the army entrusted to my care and command be provided for in a manner becoming to our government and people.

"The life of the army on the frontier is sufficiently uninviting under the most favorable circumstances and I cannot be made to believe that on the plea of a small economy, the Honorable Secretary of War, the government or our people, desire to add to its inconveniences and privations by condemning it to live in habitations scarcely better furnished than the negro quarters of the more humane and respectable portion of Louisiana sugar plantations."

Continual complaints about the food led Garnett to convene a board of survey, August 15, at the subsistence warehouse. Members of the board—Captain Archer, president; Captains Black and Frazer, First Lieutenant Carr and Assistant Surgeon Heger, recorder—found reason for the complaints. Six half-barrels of pork packed according to brand in Boston and invoiced to the post from Fort Dalles on June 12 at 11¼ cents per pound were in good condition. But 18 barrels packed partly in New York and partly in Jeffersonville, Missouri, and invoiced at 21 cents per pound were of a quality "different from what the brands warrant it to be . . . tainted and rusty," and, in an experiment made by the board, showed a "loss of about 60 per cent in cooking." Considering the quality unfit for issue to the troops, the board recommended this pork be sold. It likewise recommended for sale 370 pounds of rancid pork packed in sacks and remaining from "last year's expedition during which it was carried on mules."

Of 15,966 pounds of bacon invoiced at Fort Dalles at 20¼ and 21 cents and "sent to this post . . . since March 1, 1857, and up to August 6, 1857," all but 100 pounds was "soft, rancid and unfit for issue." The sale of the condemned pork was recommended.

Ham, in the quantity of 1,876 pounds, at 21 cents, was found to be good in original quality and present condition, as were 149 sacks of flour, costing $9.50 a barrel; three barrels of cornmeal at 5¼ cents a pound; 50 bushels of beans, at $3.90 a bushel; 1,250 pounds of rice, costing 11 and 8 cents a pound. The appraisal of 1,341 pounds of hard bread, which cost 9 cents a pound, was: "Original quality supposed good, present condition old and hard but as good as can be expected due to conditions." Two lots of coffee—1,423 pounds—costing 15½ cents a pound and received in June and August from Fort Dalles contained "many bad grains" and were rated 20 per cent below standard.

The original quality and present condition of 2,524 pounds of sugar invoiced at 12½ cents a pound—a June 12 shipment—were good, but 3,212 pounds priced at 15¼ cents and received in August were declared of "inferior quality" yet "not sufficiently so as to authorize a change in issue." Three hundred and seven gallons of vinegar, at 40 cents a gallon, by an August 13 invoice, were found good in quality but not of the brand indicated.

Brought in "by various trains between the fifth of June and third of August, 1857," 355 pounds of white soap costing 8 cents per pound were held to be "far inferior to the ordinary standard of resin soap." The board recommended that it be turned over to the post quartermaster "to be used by him as he may deem proper for various purposes." Three hundred and fifty pounds of brown soap received during the same period crumbled "at a light pressure or fall and, more than that, twice the quantity is required to effect the same amount of washing as from ordinary good resin soap." The board recommended its issue "at 100 per cent discount," as not worth a penny of the cost price of 8 cents a pound.

Sperm candles—346 pounds at 55 cents a pound—were pronounced of original quality but not "sperm" candles. Completing the inventory and passing inspection were: 22 barrels of salt ($1.50 per barrel); 527 pounds of dried peaches (at 28 cents), 395 pounds of dried apples (at 15 cents), 26 bushels of potatoes (at $2.50) and 63 gallons of molasses (at 96 cents).

For the inferior quality and bad condition of specified stores the board attached no blame to Second Lieut. Jesse K. Allen, acting commissary subsistence officer, but felt the responsibility rested "more or less with the purchasing officer." Upon accepting the board's findings, Garnett directed the post adjutant, Second Lieut. James B. S. Alexander, to sell at public auction at Fort Simcoe the stores condemned by the board, and to "cause timely notices of sale to be given at The Dalles, Vancouver, Cascades and Portland." A copy of the survey proceedings was sent to the acting commissary of subsistence at the Fort Dalles depot, with a request that he "replace with good stores the deficiency in the supply for the winter thus caused by the action of the board."

The survey was hardly out of the way when preparations had to be made for the general court martial which the commandant had been urging as essential to discipline. Capt. (Brevet Maj.) Pinckney Lugenbeel, Ninth Infantry, and Lieut. Henry C. Hodges, Fourth Infantry, were sent from Fort Dalles to serve on the court and another officer accompanied them as a visitor. The proceedings lasted five days. The day after adjournment on August 29 three enlisted men deserted. Two stole horses and the third stole $116 from a civilian carpenter. The deserters had a good start and were only caught by Lieutenant Allen and party, Major Garnett reported, "after a tedious search and pursuit of five days."

Punishment for desertion was sufficiently severe to compel a soldier entertaining the idea to think it over carefully or to speed him on his way toward the western passes or the gold fields or wherever fancy lured him. Typical is this entry in a Guard Report Book regarding a Company G private sentenced for desertion, from the findings of a general court martial, to: "Hard labor, Ball & Chain, 2 yrs & 6 mo. $5 forfeit pay each mo. Expiration of this sentence to be dishonorably discharged." Slightly luckier was an associate with two counts against him. He only had to wear a ball and chain one year for desertion and for "unsoldierlike conduct," to carry a sand bag from reveille to retreat for one month and spend two months at hard labor.

For conduct prejudicial to the service one might expect 15 to 30 days at hard labor, plus a forfeiture in pay of $5.00 or more, or receive a sentence reading: "Five days walking a ring 30 feet in diameter, carrying a log weighing 24 pounds, each alternate hour." If the court were inclined to be tough, circumstances, of course, warranting, the five days might be ten.

On a flyleaf of the last Guard Report Book used at Fort Simcoe there is inscribed: "Captain H. M. Black is a bigoted and selfish man." That obviously was from a prejudiced pen. It couldn't have been written by Pvt. Francis Jordan, for the captain put in a good word for him to the department adjutant, on October 21, 1857, as follows: "In consideration of the uniformly good conduct of Private Francis Jordan of Company G 9th Infy in confinement of which I have been a close observer since May last, I would respectfully recommend a remittance of the unexpired portion of that part of his sentence which relates to 'hard labor with ball and chain in charge of the guard and a forfeiture of $5 of his pay per month for six months.'"

Written in the Report Book: "The officer of the day and the

guard will see that the sentences . . . are faithfully executed without alteration or abatement.'' It was directed: ''The Clock in the Guardhouse shall be regulated by the Clock in the hqts office.''

Charged to the guard at one point were eight axes, three spades, four rakes, twelve balls and chains, one mallet, one shackles set, clock and case, two padlocks and keys. And guard posts (and places where this equipment was used) were listed in November 1858 as guardhouse, new corral, old corral, officers quarters and prisoners. For the guard mounted on November 15 and relieved on the 16th, the password was Wolfe and the countersign Quebec. Countersigns included Portland, Cascades, Fort Dalles, Vancouver, Salem, Benicia, Moscow, Harrisburg, Lisbon, Yorktown, Alps, Bath, Hamburg, Dover, Calcutta, Reading, Chester, New York, Winchester, Santa Fe, Vienna. (Sgt. R. Tupper, Company I, Ninth Infantry, commanding the guard, signed the last entry at Fort Simcoe, May 27, 1859.)

Meanwhile, aspects of the military life at Fort Simcoe received comment from quite different direction. Expenses of a frontier Indian war and new posts ran high, and Maj. Osborne Cross, Quartermaster Department, reporting from San Francisco, August 19, 1857, on his inspection of posts in Oregon and Washington Territories, commented on Simcoe construction and costs.

''They worked under many disadvantages,'' Cross explained, ''having nothing but what was sent from The Dalles, and all that time by Pack-trains. To get the troops under cover a large force was required: mechanics, as well as extra-duty men, had to be called into requisition; and located as they are—being required to haul their timber over two miles, and saw it at a public mill that will not cut over 1200 feet per day—the expenditures are not so very large as many may think.

''At this post the only object I could notice was a building for the Commanding Officer's quarters much larger than necessary, which was planned during Maj. Garnett's absence from Fort Simcoe. There was a large number of mechanics and extra-duty men on the rolls of the A.A.Q. Master, but unless this is resorted to the troops, both officers and soldiers, must remain unprotected from the weather as they were last year.

''This post will cost a larger sum to keep up, and if the necessity does not justify the expense, and the amount of money to be expended is to be considered before a Commanding General can establish a post, or make a move with his army against an enemy, let the first consideration be to calculate cost, before a move is made or a building erected."

Quarters then complete and under way he listed as follows: "Subaltern Officers' Quarters—two buildings, 40 feet by 25, two rooms in each building, dimensions 25 by 20 feet; Commanding Officer's Quarters—frame up. Front 56 ft. 10 in. by 31 ft. 10 in.; wing 31 ft. 10 in.; Two Buildings—Officers' Kitchens, 15 feet by 20; Two Buildings—Company Quarters, 60 feet by 25; Two Buildings, nearly complete—Company Kitchens, 50 feet by 15, each dining room 15 by 30, Kitchens 10 by 15; one Guard House, 30 feet square; two Blockhouses, 25 feet square; one Blockhouse, 25 feet square (nearly complete); Hospital Building, frame up, 50 by 25; Sawmill, frame complete; Commissary store, frame nearly up, 60 by 25."

Employed were 18 carpenters at $4.00 per day, one carpenter at $130 a month, one cook, $80 per month; one packmaster, $4.00 per day; four herders at $30 per month; one expressman, $105 per month, and 54 extra duty men. Fuel was cut and hauled by fatigue parties, forage hay was cut by extra duty men at $5.00 per ton, oats were supplied by Captain Jordan, Fort Dalles, and hay was used for straw. Sawed lumber (pine) was cut at the public (post) mill at a cost of $30 per thousand, and some was hewed at $20 per thousand. The cost of bricks made at the post was $8.00 per thousand.

Restored kitchen in CO's quarters above; and below, CO's office on second floor. (James S. Rayner photos, H. D. Guie Collection.)

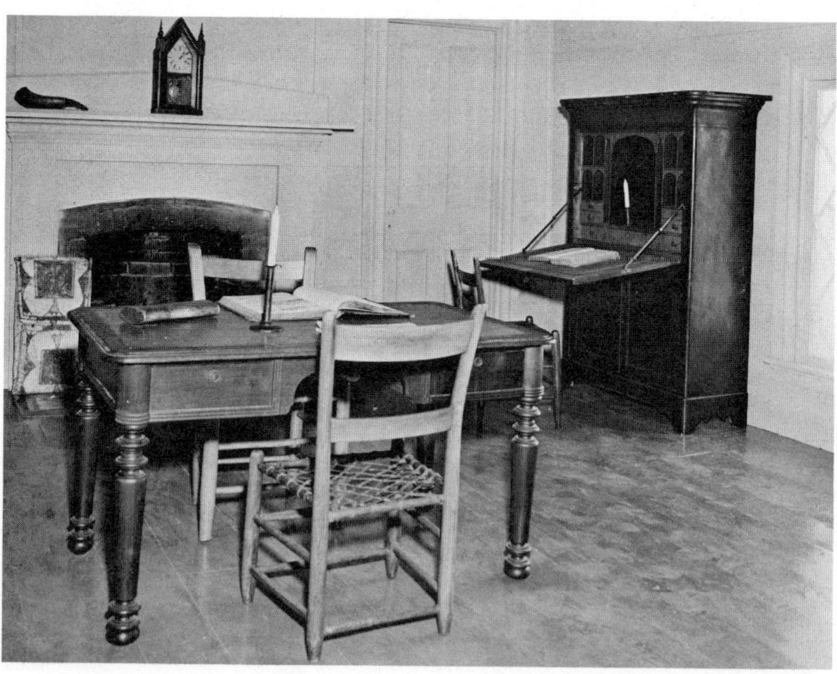

Interior views of restored Commanding Officer's quarters: above, parlor, with water color copies of portraits of Major and Mrs. Garnett; below, diningroom. Furnishings are not original. (James S. Rayner photos, 1957.)

Officers' row, Fort Simcoe, 1969. (P. Knuth photo.)

Quartermaster warehouse at southeast corner (above), with part of blockhouse at right. (Arthur E. Griffin, 1910). Log barracks below (about 1900), southeast angle of parade ground. (Mrs. H. K. Owens. Both H. D. Guie Collection.)

Irrigation, Gold, Guns

IRRIGATION came to Fort Simcoe in September, 1857, and also what looked like the making of a gold rush. A workman on a dam being constructed under Captain Archer's supervision two miles west of the post, near the outlet of the canyon where Mool-Mool Creek sinks into the ground, dug up a $20 nugget. Color had been found along the stream but that was the best showing yet. It stirred the dam builders to remarkable activity. However, dreams of another El Dorado soon faded, for there was no more pay dirt. But the reservoir was a solid achievement, and the water sparkling in the long, shallow ditch to the post held promise of flourishing company gardens the next year, a greensward, and a pond full of ice for cutting that winter. Traces of the ditch remain.

Word was received on the 27th that Lieut. Henry Douglass, on detached service with the northern boundary commission, was detailed to West Point as instructor in drawing. The lieutenant, not long after his new assignment, took as his bride Miss Isadora Bowman, the daughter of the late Capt. Francis Bowman.

Between the labors of the infantrymen and the two dozen carpenters through the summer, construction of the fort was so far along by October 1 that Archer could write to his mother: "Our post now, although not one of the buildings is entirely finished, presents the appearance of a smart village." Yet to be painted their Army sand yellow with chocolate brown trim, the quarters and other frame structures likely looked as pretty among the oaks as in agency and later years of white.

On October 22, Archer obtained his long desired leave to go

Lieut. William Myers was brevet brigadier general in 1865, retired as lieutenant colonel in 1883. (Courtesy Edward B. Page.)

home to Baltimore, and it was not until in June of 1858 that he rejoined his command. Another fall departure was that of Lieut. William Myers of Company G, anxious to get home to Cincinnati beause of Mrs. Myers' poor health.

Major Garnett received an interesting communication on October 23—General Order 13—directing the issue of the new rifle musket to regiments of the Army. The new arm had been under production since early in the year, in conformity with the program outlined by Secretary of War Davis in his report of December 1, 1856.

Davis had said then: "The operations at the national armories have been restricted to the completion of new models for small arms; the alteration of old models to long-range rifled guns, and to the preparations requisite for the exclusive manufacture of the adopted new model, of which many parts have been fabricated. This model, which is common in its general principles to all our small arms, is a rifled arm (such as is commonly called the Minie rifle) with the improvement of a lock, after Maynard's plan, self-priming, when used with the Maynard primers, and as well adapted to use with the percussion cap as the ordinary percussion lock. The alteration of flint lock to rifled arms, with the self-priming lock, has been effected to the limited extent which the means available for the purpose would allow. The results of trials with these arms leave no doubt of the propriety of the measure, which I heretofore recommended, of altering all the old model arms of the United States, including those distributed to States and Territories, by converting them into rifled arms, with the percussion self-priming lock, so as to make them conform to the new model." He further stated that "the alteration of arms of the old model, so as to apply to them all the modern improvements, has been commenced and has progressed far enough to show conclusively that they can be made equal in efficiency to those of the new model. There is in the United States arsenals, and in possession of the States, upwards of half a million of these arms, which have cost between six and seven millions of dollars."

But the Ninth Regiment would not receive the new rifle musket before it took the field again. Following receipt of General Order 13, Colonel Wright requested of department headquarters that the Ninth be permitted to retain its old Yaeger rifle, "the best arm I have ever seen in the hands of a foot soldier." That was his estimate of it before and after his '58 campaign against the "northern Indians," as set forth in his observations on material used in the expedition. The only defects he noted in the rifle were the guide sights and bayonet studs, which, he said, could be easily remedied by making them stronger.

As for the rifle muskets, the colonel commented, they had a long range and shot with great accuracy but had many defects—"they are unnecessarily long, they have not a sufficient weight of metal, the boards are too thin to admit of their being converted into rifles without danger of bursting, several have burst during the campaign, they are not near as good a weapon as the rifle of the Ninth." The Yaeger rifle (from the German *jaeger)*, also known as the Harper's Ferry rifle and sometimes as the Mississippi rifle, was the first American infantry rifle having a percussion lock. It was the regulation 1841 model.

Cabinet with pull-out writing desk (designed by Louis Scholl) in CO's parlor. Probably Mrs. Garnett wrote her letter there. (Gladys Seufert photo, 1969. OHS Collections.)

Marianna's Letter

IN the bright, scented spring of 1858, Mrs. Garnett wrote a long and chatty letter. In 1939, from a New York stamp dealer, and in the original envelope, it came into the hands of a Vancouver, British Columbia, philatelist, G.P. Bainbridge, who kindly supplied photostatic copies to this narrator.

Addressed to "Mrs. Charles Evans, Care of Lyman A. Spalding, Esq., Lockport, New York," it was a letter such as any young woman of education, position and gentle nature might pen in happy communion with a dear and distant friend. The tone of it reveals a buoyant spirit and, despite some yearnings, a ready acceptance of life on a far frontier befitting a helpmate of an Army man. Reading it, with the knowledge of the fate so soon in store, one cannot resist saying, "Poor Marianna!"

Fort Simco W. T., April 29th 1858
My dear Friend,

Your kind letter reached me two weeks since and I know not how to thank you for it. Words are but cold and vain to express the delight and pride I felt in receiving it, giving me proofs of a friendship which I have long valued but never had I thought you could feel so much interest in me as your letter tells me you do.

I am quite sure that you could not regret the loss of the letter mailed to you by the Central American as much as I did, not that it was valuable in itself only so far as you might know that in spite of the immense distance which divides us and the entire change of life to me, you had not been forgotten or the less thought of, for I assure you it seemed a real neglect on my part

Bay window in Fort Simcoe CO's quarters. (Gladys Seufert photo, 1969.)

in not writing you before leaving New York now more than a year ago.

Age must certainly be coming upon me as the years fly by very swiftly and I have heard it said as we grow older time seems much shorter than we have been accustomed to feel. I am so far removed from all of my immediate friends that sometimes I think perhaps I love them more on that account and in calling them around me in imagination none do I seek with more affection than you, for I have always held such admiration as acute a love for you and tried in many things to imitate the example I so love.

And now I must tell you of my little boy, of whose birth I trust you may have already heard. The little fellow is now 10 weeks old and a nice fat, happy and healthy child. He has dark blue eyes and a fair, clear complexion bearing no resemblance to anyone that I can see. We call him Arthur Nelson as the Major would not consent to have him named for him and I did not fancy Nelson alone. The first few weeks after the little fellows birth, I was extremely weak but in every other respect very well and I am now as well as ever and in much better general health than you have ever known me. The long sea voyage from New York to San Francisco has entirely cured the Neuralgia from which I suffered and I expect now to live to be a fat and healthy old lady. There are only two ladies here besides myself, Mrs. Black whose husband is one of the Capts. stationed here and Mrs. Heger the surgeon's wife. Mrs. B. came from N.Y. with us and we three are very social, meeting often and without much ceremony. The officers are all very agreeable and gentlemanly, make very pleasant visits and the common interest which binds all army people together makes us at a frontier post very friendly one towards the others. I have now had recently a year's experience of what is called army life though I have not experienced any greater inconvenience than one might meet with in civil life. Our mail comes but once a fortnight and then we look with such eagerness for it bringing news always, and to me good thus far. I have many correspondents and all have been very faithful but my letters must be droll affairs as of a necessity they are egotistical relating entirely my own pursuits. The Major is in command here consequently all strangers coming to the Post are our guests unless . . . invited by one of the other officers and last summer we had two Court Martials each of which sat nearly two weeks and several official visits so you see we are not without society even if we are in the midst of a wilderness.

I like housekeeping quite well and am very fortunate in service. The woman I brought is a daughter of one of the Major's uncle's house servants and although she was free, seems to think that she belongs to us, which I assure you is a great blessing.

The Major has built the Post and of course we feel particularly interested in it on that account. The house we occupy is very pretty and conveniently arranged and most happy should I be if it was situated in a more accessible place where I might have the pleasure of a visit from you, but I live in hopes that some day "The Powers that be" may send us to a pleasant and accessible Post, then I shall trust to return in a measure the kind hospitality I have received from you. Many times I think over the agreeable hours I have spent with you and particularly those past beneath your pleasant roof in Lockport and believe me I regret it extremely to heart that we should in all probability never meet there again. I am sorry for you to make a change of residence, but you must indeed feel grateful for the good fortune of still being so near your mother, Mrs. Lainerely. Most sincerely I trust that your dear husband may have succeeded in his new office as well in all respects as he could desire and that you may soon learn to like your new home more than you anticipate. Do not fail to write me full particulars on this subject and rest assured that you can not weary me by minute details relating to yourself or by the length of your letter. The longer the better. If you could look in upon us on the arrival of a mail and watch with what delight we receive letters from our friends in the 'States' you would be fully repaid for the effort of writing. I am very glad you had so pleasant a visit in Albany and it must have been a great treat for your boys. I suppose they have forgotten me by this time and I wish they could not for I am sufficiently vain to desire the remembrance of children even. We were both pleased to hear the good news of Mrs. Geo. Evans and Miss Redfield and of your brothers. The ladies you know are friends of the Major's and he is slightly acquainted with your brothers David and George. I am very much obliged to Jeannie and her husband for their kind remembrances of me and I beg you will give my "affectionate regards" and please remember me very kindly to Dr. and Mrs. Casey.

I wish you were here this lovely morn to enjoy the fine weather and beautiful flowers. It is a strange thing that the climate of this region so far north (further north than Maine) should be so much warmer and the seasons earlier than on the Atlantic.

We have had June weather, such as you have in that month at Lockport, for 4 weeks or more, and the fields and hills are covered with wild flowers many of them, fragrant and really plentiful. We reached here the 1st of May last year and I think the Spring months in this climate are the most delightful of the year, as in the summer we have very little rain and few flowers, but the true picture is even then very pleasant.

You will be in the full enjoyment of summer and all that it brings when this reaches you. The long distance I am from

Mother and Father is the greatest trial I have to bear and notwithstanding my good fortune in all other respects I do long most heartily for one moment with them. I am still a great baby when thinking of my dear parents and I sometimes wonder if the new ties and cares married life has brought will never cure me of the other childishness I still retain in my relations to them. My old friends can never be forgotten for the new ones chance may gain for me and I look forward to a happy reunion with those I have left and most heartily hope that kind fortune may grant us some happy and merry time together. I shall think of you pleasantly situated in Buffalo until I hear the contrary and do write me soon and let me know all that interests you and yours. Your sister will miss you as much as you may her, but then when you can be together you will have a greater pleasure than ever.

I hope that this lengthy and dull letter will not frighten you from writing very soon again and as much as last time. I have been obliged to write very hurriedly as I have many others to answer by this mail which leaves on Saturday and as we have an express but once a fortnight I do not like to put off answering some letters I received before my baby was born. I shall look for others from you with the greatest pleasure and if you can feel any pleasure in receiving such as I may be able to send you I shall feel very happy.

The Major desires to be kindly remembered to both yourself and husband and my best regards to him. If he will bring you out here to make us a visit we can offer him fine trout fishing and Grouse, Ducks and much other game in abundance with plenty of company to hunt with and a right good welcome. Please give my kind love to your mother and sister and remembrances to your brother, your father may not recollect me but kind regards to him also.

Master Arthur is making some sounds which call me so in mercy to you as well as duty to him will say Goodbye for a time trusting that all may be well with you and in sincere love,

Believe me truly your friend,
Marianna E. Garnett

Section of "Skeleton Map of Washington Territory . . . Compiled by G. Sohon under the direction of Lieut. John Mullan U.S.A., Ft. Dalles O. July 4th, 1858." (National Archives.) Far from Simcoe was decisive battle of Four Lakes in Wright's 1858 campaign, Sept. 1, 1858, at location south of "Fishery" on Spokane River (north of present Cheney and about 15 miles south of Spokane).

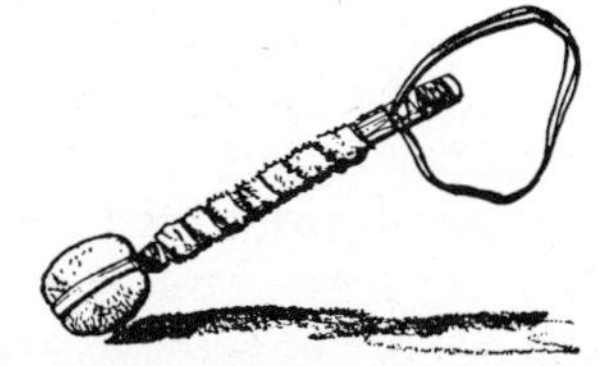

Spoiling for a Fight

MATTERS were shaping toward the showdown with the treaty tribes during the spring of 1858. Stirred by war-thirsty chiefs, who were emboldened by the forebearance of the military and not content to let well enough alone, the young men were making mischief. Palouse raiders took some government cattle in the Walla Walla Valley and two miners were reported killed on the road to Colville. Forty alarmed residents of that neighborhood petitioned Col. Edward J. Steptoe for protection. On May 6 he set out north from Fort Walla Walla for the Colville region, not to fight but to show the uniform with 152 men—Companies C, E and H of the First Dragoons, commanded, respectively, by Brevet Capt. Oliver H. P. Taylor, Second Lieut. William Gaston and Second Lieut. David McM. Gregg, and 25 men of Company E, Ninth Infantry, with two mountain howitzers, under Capt. Charles S. Winder.

North of the Snake River the command encountered 1,000 or more warriors, stripped and mounted for battle—Spokanes, Palouses, Coeur d'Alenes and some Yakimas. The chiefs parleyed in fierce humor, indicating they might contest the way, and on the following morning, May 17, launched an attack on the rear guard as Steptoe started his 80-mile retreat. It was a fatal mistake for the hostiles. While they brutally whipped the soldiers in an all-day fight near the present Rosalia, they invited the concentration of forces that would crush them before the first frost.

Steptoe's losses were seven dead, 18 wounded and one missing. Among the killed were the brave Taylor and the heroic Gaston. The enemy characteristically suspended operations at nightfall and the command managed to slip away without pursuit. But the pack train and howitzers were lost and the dead left behind, buried after darkness on the field. Had two of the dragoon companies been better armed than with their short-range musketoons, and had the inadequate supply of ammunition not run low, the affair might not have been so ruinous.

Around Simcoe things were quiet, as Captain Archer found on returning from his long leave, but he had half-expected otherwise. Upon arriving at Fort Vancouver by steamer from San Francisco on June 8, he learned of Steptoe's defeat, and he barely had begun to enjoy the warm hospitality of Fort Dalles when word came in that hostiles were assembled in force at the Klickitat Valley blockhouse where relays of horses and mules were kept. Major Lugenbeel started with a company for the relief of the little, two-story log fort, and Archer, deciding he should get back to his command, overtook the column 20 miles out and continued on alone to the blockhouse. There he was greeted by the lately commissioned Second Lieut. Elisha E. Camp,☆ who had been sent down with 15 soldiers from Simcoe by Major Garnett to alert the people at the way-point to catch, if possible, a small party of Yakimas. The Indians—two chiefs and eight followers—Garnett learned, had slipped into the valley to steal horses and cattle belonging to the government and friendly Klickitats and to incite the "friendlies." The scare, Archer commented, was an "exaggeration."

When Lugenbeel came up, he gave part of his company to Camp and ordered the lieutenant to escort a wagon train, which had been waiting at the blockhouse, on to Simcoe. Archer tarried to have dinner with the major and caught up with the train at a small stream named after the ill-fated Captain Bowman. He had tea with Lieutenant Camp and, accompanied by a soldier, started at sunset for Simcoe 40 miles distant. He preferred to travel after dark because his eyes pained him. Within 12 miles of the post, he and his companion left the road for an old Indian trail, the Eel Trail of legend, and zigzagged down it's precipitous course by light of the stars and were "heartily glad" to reach the bottom. They rode into the post "at 3 o'clock in the morning before anybody was out of bed except the sentinel."

Pleased to see the company gardens thriving under irrigation

Col. Edward J. Steptoe's defeat in May, 1858, brought more decisive than 1856 Army campaign later that year.

from the dam built at his direction the previous September, the captain said that in addition to all kinds of vegetables his own company's garden would yield "five thousand head of cabbages and two thousand bushels of potatoes which I think may be depended on to keep the scurvy from the company."

The Fraser River gold strike in the British Possessions was drawing thousands of miners—the majority going by boat to Victoria but hundreds of others by land. The Dalles, for the latter, was the principal jumping-off place. A company of 76 Californians paused at Simcoe in early June. They had all the marks of a hardy lot, were well-armed and had a captain and the semblance of a military organization. From the post they took the route of Wright's 1856 expedition. After crossing the Wenatchee River, some 100 miles by trail from Simcoe, they were attacked by Indians. The Klickitat guide deserted. One of the party was killed, two were drowned recrossing the Wenatchee, one accidentally shot himself dead and one died of fright. Pursued for two days of their four-day retreat, they lost their pack animals and most of their gear. They straggled into the post on June 26 with seven wounded, who were placed in the hospital. But gold was still in their eyes and they declared that the Wenatchee River and We-wi-wilch Creek were "richer in gold than any place in California."

Reporting to General Clarke, just arrived at Fort Vancouver from Benicia Barracks, Major Garnett said that assertedly among the estimated 100 attackers were "Owhai, his son, Qualchin, Quin-ti-neme [Quiltenenock—killed in the fight], Kut-a-cote and Skloom." In his judgment, "the Indians had no just provocation for their conduct toward the miners." Capping the ferocious assault on Steptoe's expedition, the roughing up of the California party intensified the Army's preparations to settle the local Indian question. General Clarke summoned Wright, Steptoe, Garnett and others to Fort Vancouver to lay out the campaign.

Meanwhile, Indians or no Indians, the hopeful argonauts were determined to reach the Fraser. The little Columbia River steamers were packed with men and animals, and by the middle of July 400 Californians were swarming The Dalles. "Maj." Robinson, who had shared the misfortunes of the gold seekers on the Wenatchee, was back at Simcoe in late July with 250 eager recruits from San Francisco and Los Angeles. The party encamped at the post several days and set out, confident of standing off marauders.

In early July, Wright and Garnett had received their orders for a two-pronged drive, but the prospect of action for many of the officers was less exciting than the real estate boom, due in main part to the gold rush. After a fling at the Fraser and Thompson River diggings, thousands of gold hunters tried their fortunes in Washington, and the resultant activity was felt in all the settlements. Catching the fever, some of the officers speculated in building lots in the new Whatcom (Bellingham), on Puget Sound, paying $200 per lot and talking of cleaning up $10,000. Wright was among several investing in The Dalles, now bursting its britches. Vancouver also was highly favored. But Captain Archer, as merely an interested observer, had the keenest appraisal, if not exactly for the eventual essential reason. "Se-at-le on the Sound," he predicted, "will be the great seaport for the mining region. It is directly opposite to the Sno-Qual-mi pass of the Cascade mountains and is I think the most accessible to the gold country." Forts Simcoe and Walla Walla were hives, and no less busy was Fort Dalles, which funneled in supplies by wagon train and additional troops.

Two companies of the Fourth Infantry—Lieut. George

Crook's☆ D of Fort Ter-Waw, six miles up California's Klamath River, and Capt. Henry M. Judah's☆ E, Fort Jones, below Yreka, northern California—reinforced at Simcoe. Crook had no liking for Judah, with whom he had served in the Rogue River War, and he surmised that the feeling was reciprocated. According to Crook, the captain was intoxicated a good part of the time and an "unmitigated fraud."

Crook was pleased when a squad of his men armed with the rifle musket—the 1822 model altered by converting the lock, rifling the barrel and adding a rear sight—outshot a Simcoe guard unit on the target range. The Simcoe lads, shooting Yaegers, which Captain Frazer had been contending were superior to the rifle musket, couldn't hit the bullseye, while all but one of the lieutenant's squad scored. Crook had drilled his men thoroughly down on the Klamath and taken them hunting to sharpen their shooting eye.

Preparations for the campaign were completed about simultaneously at the two advance posts. Colonel Wright started his first units from Walla Walla on August 7 and followed shortly with the main command, pointing for the Coeur d'Alene mission, in the region of which he expected to find his enemy gathered. Wright had 570 men—Companies C, E, H and I of the First Dragoons, A, B, C, K and M of the Third Artillery, and B and E of the Ninth Infantry, and a company of 30 uniformed Nez Perces.

Major Garnett swung out on the tenth, advising Vancouver headquarters he proposed to follow the familiar route of the '56 expedition, which was that of the California miners, to the "Wenatcha," thence down to its mouth, up the west bank of the Columbia to the Hudson's Bay Company's old Fort Okanogan, along the north bank of the Columbia, crossing opposite the mouth of Spokane River, striking then for Buckland Rapids and there recrossing the river and returning to Fort Simcoe. He thought it would be a good idea if Wright struck first for Lake Coeur d'Alene, then marched "straight to Colville, thence down the southern bank of the Columbia to the mouth of the Spokane and thence straight for Walla Walla." The major had not been apprised by the time of his departure north where Wright specifically planned to go, and the fact bothered him somewhat. As he commented to Major Mackall, Clarke's adju-

Gen. George Crook, about 1868, about the time of the Snake War, when he was in charge of the District of the Lakes. (OHS Collections.)

Henry M. Judah, brigadier general in this post-1862 photo. In the Pacific Northwest Crook thought him an "unmitigated fraud." (National Archives.)

tant, in a final message: "In certain cases this information might be useful to me."

Garnett's command consisted of Crook's Company D, Fourth Infantry, 79 enlisted men, whose first lieutenant, James K. McCall, was assigned to Company G of the Ninth for the campaign, leaving Second Lieut. Thomas E. Turner with Crook; and three rifle companies of the Ninth—Company C, Capt. John W. Frazer, Second Lieut. Jesse K. Allen, 73 men; Company G, Capt. Henry M. Black, 78 men; and Company I, Capt. James J. Archer, Second Lieut. Elisha E. Camp, 76 enlisted men. The total—eight line officers and 306 men; Assistant Surgeon C. C. Keeney was the medical officer. Turner was adjutant of the command and Allen its quartermaster.

Garnett had requested 30 to 50 dragoons for flankers and scouts but they were denied him so he mounted 10 men from each of the Ninth's companies under Allen "to perform exclusively cavalry service." Maintaining the column on its scheduled 50-day campaign required 225 pack animals—mules and horses, including eight for ammunition, seven for camp equipage and two for hospital stores. There was a packer for every seven mules and, altogether, 50 packers and herders.

Captain Judah, Lieutenant Alexander and Assistant Surgeon Heger, with 73 men of the captain's company, were left as a garrison. Judah managed that, said Crook, "with his usual ability to escape work," by exchanging places with a company of the Ninth and "signaled the kindness shown to him by Maj. Garnett by being drunk pretty much all the time during our absence."

Garnett was spoiling for a fight. That he didn't get one while Wright had a big one and a smashing victory was not his fault. He made all the proper dispositions, and his thoroughness would have been turned to good account had opportunity offered. By his Post Orders 17 and 25, August 5 and 9, all the likely contingencies of Indian warfare were covered, and all the details as to traveling and camping routine.

The companies of the Ninth left behind their bayonets. Officers dispensed with their swords and provided themselves with rifles and revolvers. Both officers and men outfitted themselves so far as practicable in "Hudson Bay shirts." The men started with three days' cooked rations in their haversacks and carried their knapsacks and blankets until, by the lightening of the ration loads, such impedimenta could be packed on the mules. Rations were issued every three days, to be cooked immediately upon being received. The entire command slept habitually on its arms. Each company took a tent with which to protect the arms in case of rain.

Infantry in single file, the 15-man advance guard riding 300 yards to a half-mile ahead and detaching flankers as the terrain demanded, and the 50-man rear guard covering the packtrain, the column must have looked businesslike to practiced Indian eyes. Unique in the picture, Lieutenant Crook walked at the head of his company. The other officers preferred the saddle to "shank's mare". It was Crook's maxim that "an infantry officer should march on foot when his men did." Save on two occasions, as hereinafter noted, he marched, as he said, "every foot of the way."

The battalion's route was virtually due north to the Kittitas Valley, with the first three days a shakedown for the long pull. Garnett took the convenient Indian trail through the singularly named low pass, *Sim-ku-ee,* into Medicine Valley and on over the Ahtanum Ridge, to camp the first night near the site of St. Joseph Mission. That was 15 miles. To the *Twi-wi-an* (South Fork of Cowiche Creek) was an easy 10 miles the second day, from sunrise to 10 a.m. The march was even shorter the third day, over the hills to Colonel Wright's old summer depot, Fort Na-chess, just above the present Eschbach Park near Yakima.

On the fourth day, the command marched into the Selah Valley, past an Indian winter resort on *Winass* (Wenas) Creek, across the "Basalt Mountains" (Umtanum Ridge) and down to the *Emtenum* (Umtanum Creek). Indian scouts reporting that several of the hostiles who had fought the miners were in a camp some 20 miles up the Yakima, Lieutenant Allen set out after dark with 15 men of his cavalry. The command hardly was under way in the morning when a messenger from the detachment said that the lieutenant had been wounded, perhaps fatally, in a pre-dawn rush on the camp. Garnett pushed his march and early in the afternoon met the detachment bearing the young officer, who died 15 minutes later.

From "Camp on the Upper Yakima River, August 15, 1858," Garnett advised Major Mackall: "It has become my painful duty to communicate to you for General Clarke's information and that of the adjutant general of the army the sad intelligence of the death of 2nd Lieut. Jesse K. Allen of the 9th Infantry who expired at this camp at half past 2 o'clock today. Lieut. Allen died the death of a soldier. He fell at 3 o'clock this morning at the moment of accomplishing a successful surprise on a camp of hostile Indians. There is reason however to fear that he was shot accidentally by one of his own men in the darkness of the hour.

"I must be permitted here to express my sorrow at the untimely end of this junior officer and to offer this officially, my tribute to his worth. He was an officer of rare energy and zeal. . . . I am of the conviction that his place will not again be easily filled in our service. His loss to the command can scarcely be underestimated."

The major continued that Lieutenant Allen's party captured 21 men, about 50 women and children, 70 head of horses and 15 head of cattle, and, he said: "Three of the men, having been recognized as participants in the attack on the miners, were shot in compliance with my general instructions on the subject." A fourth was shot in attempting to run when the camp was surprised, and another was found and killed later.

Lieutenant Allen's commander and personal friend, Captain Frazer, and a small mounted escort carried the body to Fort Simcoe. His body later was moved to Oak Grove Cemetery, Hillsboro, Illinois.

A 16-mile march on August 16 took the command to Lake Cle Elum—spelled *Kle-allum* and *Cleallum*—where high mountains, thickly green with pines and firs, sloped to the pebbly shores of the cold and crystal clear water. Sportive swims banished the grime and fatigue of the day, and cheerful around their fires were the men that night. But there could be no lingering at the pleasing spot. The ringing echoes of the bugles at reveille, at an hour and a quarter before sunrise, warned that it would be "Forward ho" again when the sun came up. Garnett was a stickler for early starts.

Even before reveille that morning, Captain Archer and a mounted party were in the saddle to explore the upper Yakima 20 miles beyond the lake. The major led the main command five miles downriver, where there was better grazing and where Archer rejoined it after a 45-mile ride. He'd seen no hostile

Indians but at the head of the lake on the return trip he found "a very pretty bell shaped flower" of his sister's "favorite blue color," which he picked and pressed to send to her.

On the eighteenth, the expedition left the Yakima and crossed the Wenatchee Mountains by the Naneum (Nanum) Trail to the Wenatchee River—two marching days. Crook then had an opportunity to try his luck at catching hostiles, several of whom were reported to be with a camp of Indians 60 miles up the Wenatchee. Riding muleback, with what saddles they could scare up, Crook and his company, guided by a pair of local natives, traveled up the Wenatchee all night (in the rain) and a good part of the next day.

Halting near the Indian village but out of sight, Crook managed to have a talk with the chief, whom he advised that it would be risky to harbor the miners' "murderers," that many people likely would be killed if there were a fight. The next day the chief assembled his followers at Crook's camp and by prearranged signals indicated each of the wanted men. Five were quickly seized and bound. Crook told them they were going to be shot for their crimes, which four admitted, with the excuse they were forced or persuaded. The fifth, a medicine man, acknowledged nothing but invoked curses on his captors. The lieutenant gave them a "reasonable time" to make their final preparations.

Crook relates in his autobiography: "This whole business was exceedingly distasteful to me, and as my 2nd Lieut. Turner rather enjoyed that kind of thing, I detailed him to execute them, which was done in the following manner. The Indians were set down in a line; twenty men were detailed to shoot them. Five of their guns were not loaded, so that no one knew whether his gun was loaded or not."*

On the twenty-fifth, the day after Crook's return, Archer and Camp were sent with 60 men to hunt three or four remaining hostiles, whose hiding place in the mountains had been reported. The lair was found but the quarry, warned, had flown.

---

*Turner, a Pennsylvanian, received his commission in the Second Artillery in May, 1857, and was transferred to the Fourth Infantry, March 17, 1858. He gained his captaincy in November, 1861, was breveted major for his performance in the Battle of Gaines Mill, Virginia, June 27, 1862, and died the following August 1.

Crook passed along this portion of the Columbia above Priest Rapids and below present Rock Island Dam. Looking across at Colockum Pass about due west of Grand Coulee. Where are Indians?

From Fort Okanogan on September 7, Garnett sent a note to Captain Judah saying he would be unable to reach Simcoe before the twentieth and that he was going after Indians who had fled to the Colville River. By then, over in the Spokane country, Colonel Wright had broken the power of the hostile tribes in two pitched battles, on September 1 and 5, inflicting severe losses and without losing a man.

Garnett found no more fugitives from military justice on his thrust into the northern region, nor did Archer on a three-day scout across the Columbia plains. Before starting homeward on September 15, the news of Wright's victory in the Battle of Four Lakes had been received, so then Garnett knew there was nothing of great importance left to accomplish. Besides, supplies were running low and the men's shoes were wearing out.

In returning, the expedition spent a night at the foot of Lake Chelan. There Crook was ordered to organize a "navy" and explore the Columbia, downstream, while the main body marched in the same general direction. Several pine dugouts had been picked up at the mouth of the Okanogan and packed along for navigating the river. Into them Crook disposed 20 of his men. The first day the inexpert canoeists experienced so many duckings that Crook feared some would be drowned. He

had the dugouts lashed together in pairs. Thereafter, although there frequently was strenuous bailing with camp kettles and mess pans, all ran the rough water and rapids without mishap.

Coming upon an Indian encampment, Crook landed. Painted and roached braves immediately appeared to claim ownership of the canoes. Stepping forward with his rifle, Crook threatened to shoot the first Indian to touch one. That sufficed for the moment. But Crook did not tarry, as the situation did not look "salubrious."

Altogether, it was a pleasant excursion and the envy of the command on foot. The scenery was "magnificent," the clear depths of the eddies teemed with salmon, and the locomotion was swift and effortless. When Crook abandoned his flotilla at Priest Rapids to rejoin the battalion, it was with many regrets. He couldn't recall ever enjoying a trip "with such keen zest and pleasure."

From Priest Rapids, the land of the Wanapums (River People), it was some 50 miles to Simcoe—to bunks, chairs and tables—warm days over the sagebrush hills and plains, with a crossing of the Yakima; a total of 45 days in the field, with 31 marching days (for the main column) and 505 miles behind them.

Never to Return

WHILE Crook was floating happily down the river, Garnett was riding south, with tragedy his shadow. An Indian courier from Fort Simcoe had failed to find him, and the major was unwarned. On September 16, a week before the expedition returned, Captain Judah forwarded to Adjutant Mackall the major's note of September 7, 1858, from Fort Okanogan, "received a few moments since," with a hurriedly penned message: "Supposing that Maj. G was within 80 miles of the Post and at the suggestion of Dr. Heger I despatched an Indian express to him from the latter on Monday 13th announcing to him the probable fatal illness of Mrs. G.

"I am pained to add that although still alive Mrs. G. is only so through the operation of stimulants and that Dr. has no hope of her recovery although there is always hope while life remains." He added a postscript, "I am and have been quite sick myself with bilious fever."

Mrs. Garnett succumbed on Friday, the seventeenth, presumably of "bilious fever." Little Arthur Nelson followed her six days later, on the twenty-third. Captain Archer related: "Both were well when we left. Maj. G. did not know that his family was ill until he was encamped 15 miles from here [Fort Simcoe]. He sent a messenger to tell his wife he would be there the next day, hungry and thirsty, as much as to say he wanted lunch postponed for himself and officers. The messenger came back immediately with the sad intelligence."

On September 24, Major Garnett sent to General Clarke's adjutant the following petition. "I am compelled to entreat of the general the indulgence of a leave of absence for sixty days with permission to apply for an extension of two months. The purpose of the request is to take the remains of my wife and child of whom I have been bereaved to the east."

Summing up, in his official report on the expedition, Garnett opined that the "successes of the Yakima and Wenatcha though small have repaid us however for the labor." But the Army had lost its excellent Lieutenant Allen—and not by enemy hand—and it had another casualty, Private Liebe of Company C, who, the major noted, "straggled behind the command and was found the next morning."

Short respite from the long march was granted Crook's Company D. It had to report to the Columbia district headquarters at Fort Vancouver, as did Captain Judah's garrisoning Company E. Preceded by Crook, who traveled by ambulance, the two companies shouldered arms for The Dalles on September 25. Crook says: "From here [Fort Simcoe] I was sent in advance in an ambulance. Our team gave out on the way, and we found a band of ponies on the way at a pond. We managed to catch some of them, get the harness on them, and made them pull us through. When I arrived at Fort Vancouver, Col. Newman S. Clarke, commanding the department, and his adjutant general were there, so I was ordered back to Fort Ter-Waw with my company." The order was at Crook's request, in his concern to harvest the company garden before the rains, but the garden had failed, as he found on arriving from the debarkation point, Crescent City.

Of Garnett, Crook said: "I don't know that I ever served under a commanding officer for whom I had such a high respect. He was strict, but just, and those who did their duty well were certain to be rewarded, while those who failed to do their duty were made to feel it. In this way the hard work was not all put on the willing officer."

In the period of waiting, Garnett had the glum satisfaction of reporting to headquarters the deaths of two Indians, one an emissary of Chief Kamiakin, the other a murderer of Agent Bolon. Now that Qualchan had been hung out-of-hand by Colonel Wright, and the father, Owhi, had been mortally shot while trying to escape, following the colonel's victories, Kamiakin was the last prominent hostile at large. He had sent an agent into the Klickitat country "with horses as presents to the friendly Indians there to induce them to open hostilities against whites,'' Garnett said. Friendly Indians who lived about the post captured the emissary and brought him in, and he was hung by Garnett's order. A few days later Mishalle (Mosheel) who had been the prime mover in the killing of Bolon, was reported to be trussed in a friendly Indian's lodge. A detail of soldiers sent to pick him up found him untied, and he was shot attempting to flee.

The Simcoes and Cascades were white with new snow when Garnett bade adieu to his officers and the just-arrived Col. Joseph K. F. Mansfield, inspector general, on October 18. Garnett vowed never to return to the post if he could help it, for there were his bitterest memories.

''I shall miss Maj. Garnett, whom on the whole I like as a commanding officer in spite of some little offences,'' Archer wrote to his mother. ''He is brave, intelligent, impartial (except toward himself) truthful and full of energy.'' Now in command, Archer moved into the commandant's quarters. He had purchased from the major, he said, ''all his table, kitchen, bed room and other furniture . . . indispensable to the officer of a post who is obliged to entertain visitors at his post.''

To Captain Archer fell the duty of executing two of the Bolon murder party, ''Stohan and Wap-pi-choh''—the Woppy and Stuchen named by White while he was Skloom's captive in '57. Learning that they were living at Priest Rapids, Archer sent 12 friendly Indians on October 15 to fetch them, and they soon swung from the scaffold improvised by wedging a stout timber between two of the oaks in the grove below the parade ground.

Garnett arrived in New York on Sunday night, November 28, on the mail steamship *Illinois* from Aspinwall, ''with the California mails, treasure and passengers brought by the steamer *Sonora* [to the Isthmus] from San Francisco.'' (New York *Herald* of November 29, 1858.)

Among officers listed from the territories was Major Steptoe, on sick leave, going home to Virginia an unhappy man. He was rankled that he had not received command of either the Wright or Garnett expedition, the latter being felt especially his due as senior to Garnett. ''We think,'' Captain Archer had said inclusively of fellow officers, ''he has been badly treated by Gen. Clarke in not being given opportunity to retrieve his fortunes,'' but the general could have been well advised to keep Steptoe in garrison.

Steptoe seemingly was suffering from a disorder first noted in 1857 by Dr. John F. Randolph, assistant surgeon. The latter worriedly wrote to the major's father, Dr. William Steptoe, that he had perceived pronounced symptoms of palsy, temporarily so incapacitating that the officer required assistance in mounting a horse or entering a carriage. Presently the major appeared recovered—until after the harrowing encounter in May of '58. In 1860 he married Miss Mary R. Claytor. On September 9, 1861, came gratifying promotion to lieutenant colonel, Tenth Infantry, but in hardly two months failing health forced his resignation from the service. He died, aged 49, near Lynchburg, April 1, 1865.

Major Garnett had confided in farewells at Simcoe that he hoped for a year's leave to visit Europe. While in New York, he was named to a board of officers to find a more economical means of administering the service in the Indian country. "Considering our own government sufficiently mean and niggardly in this respect already," he remarked in his own military record, "I got excused from this service."

He had sharp words for Sen. Jefferson Davis of Mississippi, past secretary of war and soon to be his president under a new flag. He advised cousin R. M. T. Hunter, senator from Virginia, to keep a close eye on the Army appropriation bill lest Chairman Davis of the Senate Committee on Military Affairs impose invidious economies. As explained to him, said Garnett in this letter of February 20, 1859, one economy sought by Davis "was intended to deprive Generals Scott, Wool and Twiggs—with all of whom Davis has quarreled—of their rations." That section, he said, and other provisions of the bill would reduce Winfield Scott's pay as chief of the Army "to a fraction over $4,000 per annum," in spite of inference or assurance by Davis that a proviso for a minimum of $10,000 would not be necessary. Further, he asserted, a part of the bill denying double rations and certain allowances when on leave of absence would fall "most heavily upon those 'hewers of wood and drawers of water' [the infantry and the cavalry] on the Indian frontiers."

He urged Hunter, "for the Lord's sake keep Davis' hands off the appropriation bill," asked if there was no way to get the

Mississippi senator off the military committee, and ventured prophetically: "If the Army and Military Academy are left much longer to his tender mercies and benevolence he will break it up entirely. I begin to think that probably that is his object."

Garnett departed, October 22, 1859, on the steamer *California* for England, and with Capt. William D. Smith, Second Dragoons, made a leisurely tour of France and Italy. Leave extended, he remained abroad until war clouds were gathering fast at home. A shipboard companion taking passage at Cork on the Cunard steamer *Arabia,* March 31, 1861, was the London *Times'* eminent war correspondent, William Howard Russell, who wrote in *My Diary North and South,* * "The Americans on board were, of course, the most interesting passengers to one like myself, who was going to visit the great Republic under very peculiar circumstances. There was, first, Major Garnett, a Virginian, who was going back to his native State to follow her fortunes. He was an officer of the regular Army of the United States, who had served with distinction in Mexico; an accomplished, well read man; reserved, and rather gloomy; full of the doctrine of States' Rights, and animated with a considerable feeling of contempt for the New Englanders, and with the strongest prejudices in favor of the institution of slavery. He laughed to scorn the doctrine that all men are born equal in the sense of all men having equal rights. Some were born to be slaves—some to be labourers in the lower strata above the slaves—others to follow useful mechanical arts—the rest were born to rule and own their fellow-men."

Marking time until Virginia would join the seceding slave states, Garnett obtained a two-week extension of his long leave. As late as the first week in April the Mother of Presidents had refused to forsake the Union, delegates to the state convention in session since mid-February voting two-to-one against separation. When the majority was reversed, April 17, by threats, coercion and blandishment, after Sumter and Lincoln's call for 75,000 volunteers to quell rebellion, and before there could be the popular vote specified in the document, the Ordinance of Secession was proclaimed.

By letter from Lloyds, Virginia, April 30, 1861, Major Garnett

*Edited by Fletcher Pratt (Harper & Brothers, 1954), p.1.

Commandant's residence, Ft. Simcoe, 1930. Agency period picket fence and cement walk over original bricks. (H. D. Guie photo.)

resigned his commission in the Army of the United States, tendered his sword to Virginia and the Confederacy, and made his final appointment with destiny. He was named adjutant general of the Virginia forces, with rank of colonel, and assigned to organizing the Virginia troops. He was commissioned brigadier general on June 6, 1861.

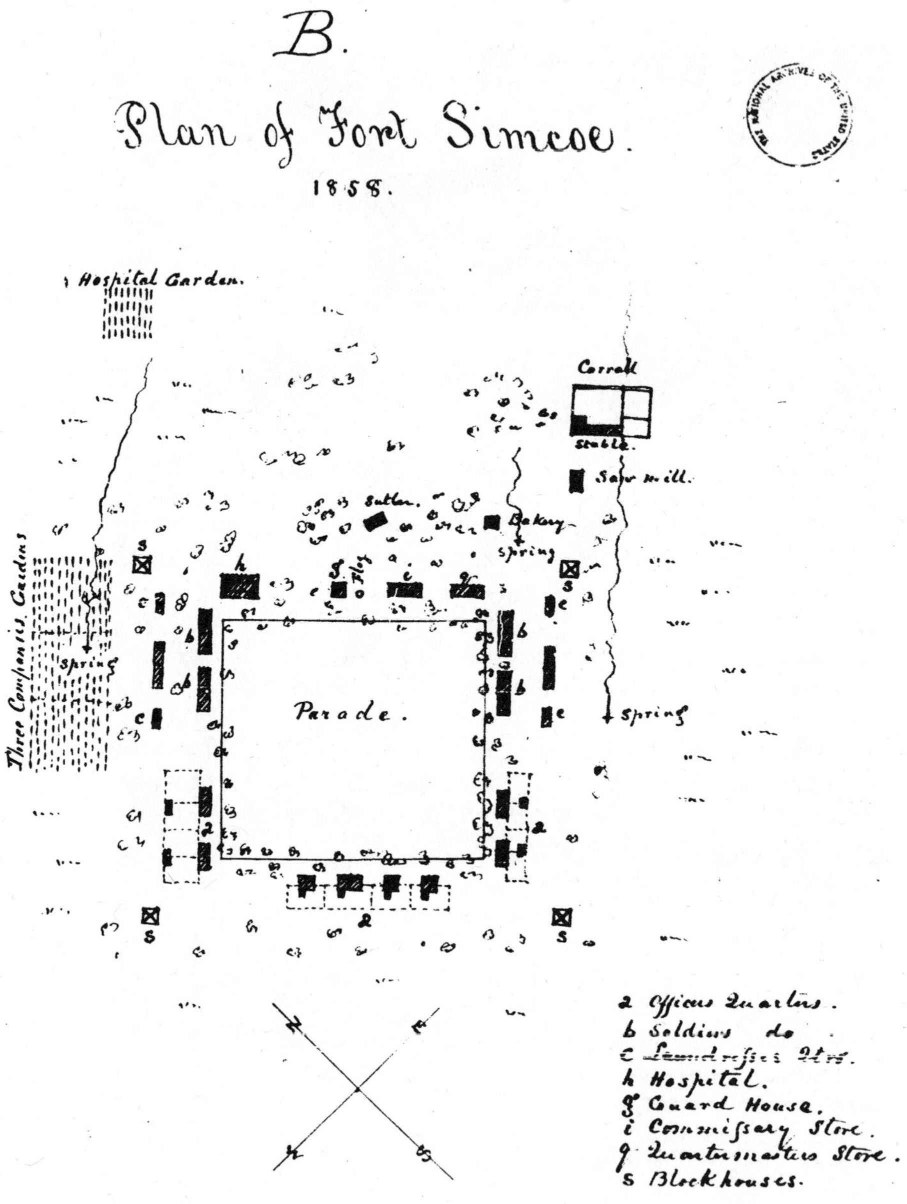

B.

Plan of Fort Simcoe.

1858.

Hospital Garden.

Corral

Stable.

Saw mill.

Sutler.

Bakery

Spring

Flag

Three Companies Gardens

Spring

Parade.

Spring

a Officers Quarters.
b Soldiers do .
c ~~Laundresses Qtrs.~~
h Hospital.
g Guard House.
i Commissary Store.
q Quartermasters Store.
s Blockhouses.

Fort Simcoe plan sent with Mansfield inspection report, October, 1858. (Roll 581, Microcopy 567, National Archives.)

Mansfield's 1858 Inspection

JUST before Garnett left Simcoe, Col. J. K. F. Mansfield arrived to begin post inspection. He had just completed similar review at Fort Walla Walla and of Wright's command just returned from the field. The inspector was at Simcoe a week and kept everybody there on the double. But the last day, he declared, should be one for pleasure, so Captain Archer "had all the ladies of the post, consisting of Mrs. Black and Mrs. Heger and little Emma Black to dinner and to spend the evening" with the staff.

As for official records, the colonel, in his "Report of the Inspection of Fort Simcoe Washington Territory, 15th to the 25th October, 1858," to Brevet Maj. Irvin McDowell, mentions arriving at Simcoe the evening of October 15. The "following morning commenced my inspection."

"I found Major R. S. Garnett in command of three companies of the 9th Inft, to wit: C, G and I. He had received a leave of absence for two months, with permission to apply for an extension for 60 days. This was in consequence of the death of his wife and child, whose remains he was about to accompany to the Atlantic states. He had made his preparations to leave that morning, and until 10 o'clock of that day he was with me affording all the information he could impart in so brief a period; and took his departure accompanied by the sympathies of those who knew his worth and could feel for his misfortunes."

Saying that Garnett "returned from the expedition after the Indian murderers the 23rd September" and was gone 45 days, Mansfield gave a daily itinerary, as reported to him by Captain Black, whose figure of the distance covered was in the aggregate "507 miles at an average of 11 miles per day."

Fort Simcoe, Mansfield said, was "situated about in latitude 47° 30' north, three miles from either of two small running streams. The Simcoe & and To-pan-ish, which unite some six miles down the valley in a northeast direction, forming the river Pisco which runs about 25 miles in this valley and empties into the Yakama river, which is indicated at the east end of the valley by a green margin, the cotton wood trees on its bank some 30 miles off.

"This peculiar strategic position is not apparent to me, altho' it may exercise an influence on the Indians east of the Cascade Mountains. It is however on no particular route to any place, and the traveling ceases when the post is reached. It is 65 miles from the Dalles, over a good mountainous road. It is accessible from Walla Walla via the Dalles with wagons, and by trail by crossing the Columbia River at [the mouth of the] Walla Walla [River] say 90 miles. It is about 90 miles through the Nachess Pass to Steilacoom . . . and about 100 miles by trail from Fort Vancouver. . . . It was placed in the midst of a small scrub oak grove with three good springs convenient, and mountain pines to any extent for building purposes obtained within ten miles; and there may be five years supply of oak wood convenient. The thermometer ranges here from 104 in summer to 20 degrees in winter, and the snow falls two feet deep.

"There is a want of rain for vegetation; yet good gardens do well, except for the attacks of crickets, which are as bad here was the grasshoppers in some other localities. The soil is very stoney thro' the whole valley, and not very rich, and the grass is not remarkably abundant, altho' enough can be cut within 10 miles for the fodder for a reasonable number of animals in winter.

"The site was selected by Col. George Wright when in pursuit of the Yakama Indians in 1856, under orders from Genl. Wool, then commanding the Department, & Major Garnett was ordered to erect buildings for 4 companies, and it was commenced the 8th August. The troops were put to work & buildings commenced on 4 sides of a square parade of 400 feet in the clear. They are judiciously arranged. . . . At the 4 corners are 4 blockhouses designed for defensive flanking of the whole. The officers & soldiers quarters are relatively well placed & the hospital & quartermaster & company stores also. The soldiers quarters are built of hewn logs & supplied with kitchens, each, and the men sleep in double bunks three tiers high; 84 men can sleep in them. Yet they are too contracted and there is not sufficient space allowed for the comfort of the men. However in the course of a year or less, this may be but a two company post, which I apprehend will be ample for this locality, and then the quarters which now exist for 4 companies will very comfortably accommodate two.

"The officers quarters, are 4 of them frame buildings and 4 log buildings, and ample for 3 companies, the command as it is now, and probably will not be extended.

"Of the 4 companies originally designed for this post Captain Woodruff's is attached to the northwestern boundary commission, and may never return here again.

"The Commanding Officer's quarters do not seem to be as judiciously planned as the others. A less fanciful building would probably have been quite as comfortable.

"The hospital is a good frame building but a little too contracted for 3 companies. Yet this is a healthy locality & I think it ample in contemplation of a two company post.

"A guardhouse of logs and 2 prisoners rooms attached are all sufficient.

"A good smith's shop, post bakery, root-house, ice-house, stables for animals well arranged, and excellent corral and hay yard.

"A good mule power sawmill supplies the lumber. The logs for it are drawn from the neighboring mountains.

"As a whole the post is very creditable to Major Garnett, who planned and superintended the building of it.

"There is a sutler's store & no liquor is allowed to be sold, an excellent regulation. Keith & Allen are the Sutlers, the same that keep the sutler establishments at the Dalles and Walla Walla. There may be an error in allowing the same persons to suttle at so many posts.

"There are three gardens, one to each company, and a hospital garden, which yield a fair supply of vegetables, melons, etc. of excellent quality notwithstanding the crickets which are so destructive at certain seasons.

"This post was built principally by extra duty men and is almost completed. There is wanted a magazine and some paint and lime and a few quartermaster supplies. Brick is made and burnt here and charcoal. Three of the officers quarters and the hospital being of planed boards should certainly be painted on the outside to preserve them. I shall call the proper attention to this subject."

Respecting "The Troops," the inspector general wrote: "Major Garnett having just left on leave of absence, the command devolved on the 16th October on the Senior Captain, J. J. Archer of the 9th Inft. The staff consisted of 2nd Lieut. J. B. Alexander 9th Inft. acting Adjutant of the post, Assistant Quartermaster and Commissary of Subsistence, of Asst. Surgeon A. Heger, and an hospital steward, who had just been tried under charges preferred by Capt. H. M. Judah, the decision of the court not known, and an ordnance sergeant. Companies C, G, I of the 9th Inft constitute the strength of the garrison."

The available force was 238 men, four officers, and included 15 sick, a corporal and six men confined; laundresses were seven. Under "Post Ordnance" were two brass mountain howitzers whose carriages required painting, a portable forge, five rifles, 14 old pattern muskets, 2500 musket ball cartridges and 1000 percussion caps, in charge of the ordnance sergeant, and canister, shells and spherical case shot for the howitzers. But, he pointed out, there was no magazine, as specified in Garnett's ground plan, and it was not subsequently built.

Of the Medical Department, Mansfield wrote: "Asst. Surgeon A. Heger is in charge with a hospital well supplied . . . and well kept, with a good hospital steward and the public stores well protected—books & records in good order & there seemed to be nothing wanted and the post remarkably healthy."

The Quartermaster Department, under direction of Lieut. James B. S. Alexander, showed post expenditures of $23,732.13 in 1857 and $33,311.38 in the three first quarters of 1858. Supplies were ample and a winter's supply of wood was on hand. "There are kept 8 horses, 58 mules, 5 wagons, 4 carts and one ambulance."

The Commissary Department, also under Alexander, had ready for forwarding $5,927 due the U. S.; $517 cash on hand and $5,410 on deposit in the Sub-Treasury, San Francisco. A chief herder was employed at $85 and a ration per month. Two Indian herders received one dollar per day and a ration. Two extra duty men were serving as commissary sergeant and butcher. Beef cost 9-5/8 cents a pound on the hoof.

Inspector General Joseph K. F. Mansfield toured the West on more than one occasion, inspecting Pacific Northwest posts in 1854, before Fort Simcoe was built. He died in Civil War. (OHS Collections.)

"The discipline of this post is good, and the post and company records well kept," said Mansfield, who reported 64 desertions from the garrison since founding of the post, G Company having the most, 27, but none in 1858. "The general appearance of the men was neat, their arms clean on inspection. Each company drilled separately, and went through the drill as skirmishers. There were many recruits that did not join in the drill. Each company fired at a target six feet high and 22 inches broad at 200 yards. Of forty men in each of Companies C and G, one-fifth struck the target, but of Company I only one twentieth struck the target. The firing was wild. The drills but fair. . . . The troops have been hitherto employed at the labor of erecting quarters, etc.

"The post guard is 13 strong and two non. com. officers, one bugler, and there were eight prisoners: two for desertion and six minor offenses."

Payment of the troops had been too slow and irregular, he suggested; the paymaster, whom he found at the post, had just reached there "for the first time since last November." Almost a full year! "Complaint was made by soldiers individually to me," Mansfield wrote, "of the long intervals between payments, which obliged them to run up long accounts with the sutler, and deprived them of funds to purchase little comforts. . . . The subject of payments I shall lay before the General commanding the Department for correction."

He concluded: "The Indians in this locality are known as the Yakama nation, and this post is on the reservation marked out by Gov. Stevens. I saw but a few lodges of them on the To-pi-nish who were quite harmless. It is here however where Major G. O. Haller of the 4th Inft was severely handled. The friendly party brought in, when I was at the post, two of the murderers of Bolan: and there is every indication of a long peace with them. They cannot be numerous, and number probably not exceeding 400 souls. I would advise they be put on a reservation & provided for as in like cases."

Bugles Blow Goodbye

INDIANS at Simcoe had predicted an early and severe winter for 1858-59, like that of 1856-57. The first snow in the hills in mid-October gave some color to their forecast and caused apprehension that the regular, bi-monthly communications with the outside would be presently cut off. But the Indians didn't have the feel, for once, and the winter in the valley was surprisingly light.

On November 10, Captain Archer sent a party of 39 mounted men under Lieutenant Alexander with orders to proceed to a point on the Columbia about 35 miles above the mouth of the Okanogan to attempt the capture of some "hostile Indians and murderers of white men." Due to the weakness of their animals, the party got only to the crossing of the Columbia 75 miles from the post. But, with the help of some friendly Indians they "succeeded in taking five Indians," said Archer, "who had murdered white men in times of peace," and returned on the nineteenth.

The captain was hopeful of having a general court martial in early December, with the idea that the officers who would have to come up from Fort Dalles might become snowed in at Simcoe and thus add to the social life of the post. Instead, on the fourth of the month, he was forced to send Captain Black, Lieutenant Camp and Dr. Heger, with five prisoners and a dozen witnesses to a general court at Fort Dalles. Likely among the prisoners was a private who had killed Sgt. John T. Osborne of Company I on November 9, as the sergeant was taking him from the company parade to the guardhouse.

The departure of the party left only Captain Frazer and Lieutenant Alexander, and Mrs. Black and Mrs. Heger for social

General W. S. Harney put an end to Fort Simcoe's army function.

gatherings, and the captain feared it would be a rather dull Christmas. But they managed well enough, and by New Year's day the absentees were back to join in the festivities. The winter continued mild, and it was not until January 11, 1859, that there was enough ice—six inches thick only—to warrant putting any in the icehouse. On the twelfth, six inches of snow fell. It soon began to melt.

Like Garnett, the captain was annoyed by the need to employ soldiers as laborers. Ever since the major had gone away, Archer had been using 20 to 80 soldiers as carpenters, blacksmiths and wood hewers, as he expected to be doing for some months. It seemed to him that the work would "never be quite done," to the detriment of proper military exercise. There came disturbing rumors that some of the companies of the Ninth would be shifted to establish posts at the old Hudson's Bay Company posts of Boise and Colville. Archer trusted that one would not be his. He thought it already "had its share of hewing wood and smoking brick and living out of doors through the winter while the houses are building."

The rumors were well-founded. On November 5, 1858, Brig. Gen. William S. Harney, now commander of the new Department of Oregon, had informed the War Department that he expected to establish a garrison in the vicinity of Colville to protect the interests of the citizens there and to serve as a check on the tribes. The War Department did not consent but Harney was persistent. On January 20, 1859, he told the department that the proposed military establishment at Colville would "dispense with the necessity of a command at Fort Simcoe as the Indians now held in check by Simcoe are more easily reached from Colville, and the difficulties to be overcome in reaching the two points are not comparable." He further suggested that the soldiers then at Simcoe and one company from Fort Walla Walla be moved to Colville and that Simcoe be turned over to the Indian Department for use as an agency.

The Northwest Boundary Commission, which soon expected to begin its 49th parallel surveys east of the Cascades, reinforced Harney's desire to abandon Simcoe. The commission asked the general for a military escort to protect its working parties. On February 7, Harney wrote to the War Department, asserting that this demand for troops "determines me to establish the post near Colville, in which vicinity they [the commission] will winter next season, and from which garrison escorts can be furnished to the different parties as they are needed."

Still unimpressed, the War Department, through the adjutant general, replied on March 18 that it was "deemed expedient to adhere to the instructions conveyed to you in my communication of 23 February 1859, touching on the location of new posts within the department of Oregon." But the adjutant general was a long way from the Pacific Coast and General Harney was inclined to solve his problems in his own way. On April 19 he informed the department that "in making the necessary arrangements for the increased escort to the northwest boundary survey, as requested by the commissioner, I have deemed it advantageous to the service to withdraw the garrison from Fort Simcoe, the necessity for its presence at that point being removed by the troops posted in its front on duty with the survey."

He continued: "This reduction will materially decrease the expense, for the maintenance of a garrison at Fort Simcoe has been and always will be at a heavy cost. Besides there is no service it could perform that cannot be done by a command from this place equally well and with more economy.

"To secure the position in the event of its being wanted hereafter as a military station for any contingency, I made offer of the use of the buildings to the superintendent of Indian affairs for Washington and Oregon, with the condition that they would be relinquished if needed for the troops. This offer has been accepted, and an agency will be established at that point under the resolution imposed. Special Orders Nos 35 and 36 from these headquarters [Fort Vancouver] copies of which have been forwarded to your office, will explain more fully the details of the above arrangements."

Thus the tough Tennessean disposed of the War Department's nonsensical notion. The old campaigner, veteran of the Black Hawk, Seminole and Mexican wars—he was breveted brigadier general for gallantry at Cerro Gordo—wasn't taking instructions that conflicted with his appraisal of the realities.

Still, by April 1, the Simcoe garrison, without anything definite to go on, was diligently working its gardens. Word had been received from Captain Ingalls at Fort Vancouver not to go to any great trouble or expense about anything because of the possibility that within three months the post would be assigned to the Indian Department. But Captain Archer had no doubt that at least one company would remain there a year longer, although recalling that General Mansfield had said in his report that Simcoe was not on any particular route anywhere.

By mid-month the hills and prairies were thick with flowers again—masses of the blue windflowers and golden buttercups sprinkled with pink sage and dotted with the little coyote eyes, and thick beds of purple violets sweetly scenting the air.

An order received at department headquarters forbidding the building of any new posts lifted the garrison's hopes that no move would be required, after all. Besides, Colonel Wright and all the other officers acquainted with the country seemed sure that Harney would not go through with his plans. But they didn't know Harney. The blow fell on April 17.

Captain Archer received his orders that day to take his Company I and Frazer's C to the 49th parallel to relieve Woodruff's company and form the escort for the boundary commission. Captain Black was ordered to Fort Dalles with Company G to relieve A and K, which Major Lugenbeel would take to Colville to establish a temporary post to protect the commission's supplies. At least, Archer's company would not be set once more to hewing timbers, nailing boards and smoking brick, which was some consolation.

With Frazer, Archer journeyed to Fort Vancouver to make certain preparations for the new undertaking, to Portland to make a few personal purchases, and to Salem. After the Simcoe winter, the Fort Vancouver sojourn was most enjoyable. It included a formal dinner at the general's establishment. An interesting arrival from the East, on the mail steamer, was former Governor Stevens, now delegate to Congress from Washington Territory.

From Simcoe on May 26 Indian Agent R. H. Lansdale wrote to Col. J. W. Nesmith, superintendent of Indian affairs, Salem, Oregon, that Captain Archer had just turned over to the Indian Department all the 21 public buildings—valued at $30,000. As Lansdale began the transfer of departmental activities from the wartime White Salmon Agency on the Columbia River to Fort Simcoe, Archer continued distribution of the garrison, begun with the departure of Company G on the eleventh for Fort Dalles. Companies C and I were started toward Fort Colville on May 28, Archer remaining overnight to complete arrangements and catching up with the battalion at Ahtanum Creek next day. Lieut. J. B. S. Alexander and a detachment of 15 were left to guard the public property yet to be removed, including stores and the portable horsepower sawmill, to be taken to Fort Dalles.

Snow blocking the mountain trails between the Kittitas and Wenatchee valleys, the Colville-bound command took a longer route. It crossed the seasonally high and swift Yakima below the mouth of the Naches, ferrying the men, baggage and provisions, and swimming the horses and mules, camped on the thirty-first opposite the mouth of the Wenas—"Camp Sela"—and marched north over the greening hills to the Columbia. By often rough and broken trail, the battalion reached the Wenatchee, lost several mules down a precipice, continued along the Columbia to the Okanogan and on to the border's Lake Osoyoos. There, at the base of summer operations for the boundary commission, camp was set up on June 19, 1859.

Fort Simcoe was another memory.

Postscript

IN JULY of 1861, Garnett of Simcoe and McClellan of *Simkwee* Creek came to grips in the rain-washed hills and valleys of northwestern Virginia. Against Maj. Gen. George B. McClellan's 9,000 operating from the rail point of Grafton on the Baltimore and Ohio Railroad to clear the western approaches to the Shenandoah Valley, Garnett had 4,000 Virginia and Georgia troops. They were largely recent recruits and few of their officers were experienced.

Garnett, Lee's adjutant, had been rushed in to save a desperate situation, following a Federal victory at Philippi, 15 miles south of Grafton. Better might Lee have risked one of his field commanders, for Garnett, to him, was considered indispensable. The newly-starred brigadier was put to a task, about the likely outcome of which he had no illusions. The night before he left Richmond to take charge of two hastily assembled advance regiments, he is recorded as saying, "They have not given me an adequate force. I can do nothing. They have sent me to my death."

With officers and men like those in the old Ninth, the odds would have been the less and they would have been reduced further by Garnett's adroitness at maneuver. But, with all their willingness, the Virginia and Georgia boys—the most of them—were too green at arms. The turning of a flank at Buckhannon Pass on July 11, resulting in the splitting of his army and the surrender of one unit of 550 men, forced Garnett to retreat from his own position at Laurel Hill into and down the Cheat River Valley with his three remaining regiments, a squadron of cavalry, a section of artillery and his wagon train.

The route of retreat on July 13 required several crossings of the swollen Shaver's (or Main) Fork of the Cheat. As he reached the second ford, Union troops caught up but Garnett stemmed the advance and saved his precious baggage train. Three-and-a-half miles further, at Carrick's (locally *Corrick's*) Ford, the last half of the train stalled in the deep water. Garnett decided to make a rear guard stand to cover the flight of his main column toward St. George. The topography was favorable for a holding action from the right bank, where a bluff commanded the approach to the ford, but the dispositions had to be made hurriedly. Valuable time had been lost trying to extricate some of the wagons. At the last minute, Garnett posted 10 skirmishers near him in some driftwood but did not take cover himself.

The firing opened as the Federal van appeared on the far side of the stream, and for a few minutes there was a brisk exchange. The skirmishers, save one, a Georgia youth, suddenly melted away. Union accounts say they incontinently fled after firing one volley.

Ignoring the Federal musketry, Garnett turned to rally the vanishing skirmishers, waving his scarf, it is said. At that moment, Sgt. Benjamin F. Burlingame, Company E, Seventh Indiana Volunteers, took deliberate aim and fired. Garnett dropped, the ball through his back, and another shot felled the plucky Georgia lad beside him.

Among the Union officers to witness was Col. (later Brig. Gen.) Robert H. Milroy, of the Indiana regiment, who, some 20 years later, as superintendent of the Yakima Indian Reservation, would live in Garnett's house at Simcoe. As they quickly came up, Maj. Gen. Thomas A. Morris, Maj. John Love and Capt. H. W. Benham, all of whom had been intimately acquainted with Garnett, recognized the figure on the sand. Major Love had been Garnett's roommate for four years at West Point.

The correspondent for the *Cincinnati Gazette* wrote: "Garnett fell instantly on his back, his head lying towards our forces, and his mouth opening wide, as if gasping for breath. He uttered not a single groan, and when Major [J. W.] Gordon reached him, scarcely a moment after he fell, his muscles were just making their last convulsive twitch. The Major stooped down, tenderly closed his eyes, bound up his face, disposed his limbs, and left him lying on the river bank, with a guard of patriot soldiers around to protect his corpse from any possibility of indignity. . . . As soon as the proper arrangements could be made, Gen. Garnett's body was conveyed on one of his own litters, thrown from their wagons by his flying soldiers to hasten their retreat, to Gen. Morris' headquarters. There fresh clothing was procured from a Georgia trunk in one of the captured wagons, and the body was decently laid out. . . .

"When Gen. Garnett fell it was only known that he was an officer attempting to rally the flying rebels. He wore a Colonel's uniform, with the epaulet changed, and the Brigadier-General's silver star glittering on the shoulder strap. Over this he wore a fine black overcoat. The ball struck him in the back (as he was turning on his heel to rally his men), passed transversely through his body, and came out on the left side of the breast. He wore a dress sword, with silverplated hilt, which had been presented by his old friend, Gen. G. M. Brooke, of War of 1812 distinction. This, with his gold chronometer, the opera glass slung across his shoulder, a fine topographical map of Virginia, and his pocket-book, containing sixty-one dollars in Virginia currency, were taken from his person by Major Gordon, to be kept at headquarters till an opportunity should offer for returning them to his family. Two or three of the bills in the pocket-book were of the new edition of continental money lately issued by Virginia."

The Georgia trooper was buried in an orchard on the hillside behind the Corrick house overlooking the ford, which is within the corporate limits of Parsons, West Virginia. * Garnett's body

*Carrick's Ford, where Garnett was killed, is a half-mile south of the Tucker County courthouse, on U. S. Route 219. The ford was named after an early settler, J. M. Corrick, who built a log house on a slope about 200 yards back from the east bank of the river. The name, *Carrick,* was used in contemporary newspaper accounts of the engagement and has persisted in most references. The spelling *Corrick* is insisted upon locally and appears on state highway markers at and near the site of the action. Close on the scene is General Garnett Post No. 4322, Veterans of Foreign Wars.

The setting is semi-rural, and it is not difficult to visualize the action in which Garnett fell. In his report of the battle, Col. W. B. Taliaferro, Twenty-third Virginia Infantry, who was a cousin of Garnett, said in part: "On the farther side of this ford I met General Garnett, who directed me to halt my regiment around the turn of the road, some hundred and fifty yards off, and to detail for him ten good riflemen, remarking to me, 'This is a good place behind this drift-wood to post skirmishers.' I halted the regiment as ordered, but from the difficulty of determining who were the best shots, I ordered Captain Tompkins to report to the general with his whole company. The was taken to the Corrick house, then occupied by William Corrick but used by General Morris as a temporary headquarters. From there it was escorted by Maj. J. W. Gordon of General Morris' staff to Grafton, where a metal casket was procured. The *Cincinnati Commercial* correspondent, who was a member of the escorting party, wrote: "In person Gen. Garnett was about five feet eight inches, rather slenderly built, with a fine, high arching forehead and regular and handsome features, almost classic in their regularity and mingled delicacy and strength of beauty. His hair, almost coal black, as were his eyes, he wore long on the neck, in the prevailing fashion among the Virginia aristocracy. His dress was of fine blue broadcloth throughout, and richly ornamented. The buttons bore the coat of arms of the State of Virginia, and the star on his shoulder-strap was richly studded with brilliants."

The *Evening Star,* Washington, D. C., July 18, 1861, reported: "The remains of Gen. Garnett, killed in the Cheat River battle, were conveyed to Wheeling on Tuesday en route

---

general, however, would not permit them to remain, but after selecting ten men, under Lieutenant Depriest, ordered the company back to the regiment.

"By General Garnett's orders, conveyed by Colonel Starke, I posted with that officer three of my companies on a high bluff overlooking the river, but finding the undergrowth so thick that the approach of the enemy could not be well observed, they were withdrawn. A few minutes after these companies rejoined the regiment Colonel Starke rode up and said that General Garnett directed me to march as rapidly as I could and overtake the main body. In a few minutes afterwards Lieutenant Depriest reported to me that General Garnett had been killed. He fell just as he gave orders to the skirmishers to retire and one of them was killed by his side."

Colonel Taliaferro gave the casualties of his regiment in the Carrick's Ford affair as 13 killed and 15 wounded. His account is from *Official Records of the Union and Confederate Armies* (Government Printing Office, 1880), Series 1, Vol. 2, p. 285.

Capt. H. W. Benham, Corps of Engineers, commanding the advance Union column, said in his formal report to Gen. Morris: "The result of this action proves to be the capture of about forty loaded wagons and teams, being nearly all their baggage train, as we learn, and including a large portion of new clothing, camp equippage, [*sic*] and other stores; their headquarters papers and military chest; also two stands of colors and one fine rifled piece of artillery; while the commanding general, Robert S. Garnett, is killed, his body being now cared for by us, and fifteen or twenty more of the enemy are killed and nearly fifty prisoners are taken. Our loss is two killed and six or seven wounded; one dangerously." (From *Official Records of the Union and Confederate Armies,* Series 1, Vol. 2, p. 222.)

for Washington City (via Adams & Co. Express). From this city they will be conveyed under flag of truce to his former home in Virginia.''

As noted in the *Richmond Enquirer,* July 27, ''The remains of Gen. Garnett reached Baltimore July 22, 1861, and was taken in charge by Messrs. Benjamin M. Garnett and C. R. Hodges, by whom it was deposited in Greenmount Cemetery to await the orders of his more intimate relatives.'' Brig. Gen. Henry R. Jackson, Garnett's successor, meanwhile had sent a flag to McClellan, requesting that the body might be borne home, to which petition the Union general readily acceded. But, the latter recalled in his memoirs, ''before my orders in the case could reach Grafton the corpse had been taken east by the father of his late wife.'' For some reason, however, removal of the body from the mausoleum in Greenmount Cemetery, Baltimore, to Green-Wood Cemetery in Brooklyn was postponed until the close of the conflict.

On Lot No. 11584/86, Section 150, Green-Wood Cemetery, there is no marker for the resting place of Robert Selden Garnett. Only the cemetery files reveal that he lies by his wife and son—poor remembrance for a distinguished soldier, the first general officer to fall in the Civil War.

Garnett's pocket compass. Lid inscription: ''Rebel Brig. Gen. R. S. Garnett, killed at Carricks ford July 12, 1861.'' Long a keepsake of William Garnett Perrow, who gave it to H. D. Guie.

Fort Simcoe parade ground, officers' row, 1941. (H. D. Guie photo.)

Among Those Present or Accounted For

Telling of some who were more or less prominent at Fort Simcoe, 1856-59, or who had a part in events pertaining to its establishment.

Brig. Gen. Robert S. Garnett, C.S.A. (National Archives.)

ROBERT SELDEN GARNETT

ROBERT SELDEN GARNETT of Virginia and Fort Simcoe was, in the classic phrase, an officer and a gentlemen. The uniform of the United States Army became him well until, out of greater loyalty to his native state and in his passion for the doctrine of States' Rights, he chose to shed it for the Confederate gray. When he fell in the first flush of the civil conflict, Southern leaders mourned for a brilliant star extinguished and former comrades in Union blue paid sad respects to a gallant enemy.

Throughout his career under the two flags of his country, Major Garnett of the United States—Brigadier General Garnett of the Confederate States of America—was beyond professional reproach. Diligent in the performance of duty, he could be trusted to do in a most soldierly manner whatever was assigned or circumstances dictated. He had exceptional military capacity —so fully shown in the war with Mexico, on the Pacific Northwest frontier and in the brief and shattered period of his devotion to the Lost Cause.

He was reserved, aloof and proud, exacting but as prompt to commend as to reprimmand, and fellow officers answerable to him could never complain of favoritism. Always a prime consideration was the welfare of his command. Such was the character and reputation of this austere, slight, darkly handsome Virginian who held the respect and confidence of subordinates and enjoyed the esteem of superiors.

Of Old Dominion first family and French lineage, Garnett was the third of seven children and the first of five sons of Robert Selden and Olympe Charlotte (de Gouges) Garnett. Two of his brothers became captains in the Confederate Army, a cousin, Brig. Gen. Richard Brooke Garnett, died in Pickett's charge at Gettysburg, and several others of collateral lines gave distinguished service to the Confederacy.

His father, a lawyer and a close friend and supporter of Andrew Jackson, served as a member of the Virginia House of Delegates, 1816-17, and as a representative in Congress, 1817-27. His mother, born in Paris, was a daughter of Gen. Jean Pierre de Gouges of the French Army and a sister of a governor of the French West Indies. Surviving her husband 16 years, she died on the day, oddly enough, that son Robert Selden undertook the building of Fort Simcoe, August 8, 1856.

Garnett was born December 16, 1819, on the family estate, Champlain, in Essex County, in the lovely Tidewater region. He was graduated from the United States Military Academy, June 22, 1841, twenty-seventh in a class of 52, for a second lieutenancy in the dragoons. Six months later, January 31, 1842, he was appointed and breveted second lieutenant in the Fourth Artillery, Company G, Oswego, New York. From early February, 1843, to October 14, 1844, he was assistant instructor of infantry tactics at the Academy. On December 26, he was appointed aide-de-camp to Gen. John Ellis Wood at Troy, New York, headquarters for the eastern division. Resigning the staff appointment the following August, he joined his company at Fortress Monroe, Virginia, and sailed with it to Aransas Bay, Texas, arriving September 26 and joining the Army of Occupation under Maj. Gen. Zachary Taylor at Corpus Christi. As adjutant of the artillery battalion, he was in the battles of Palo Alto and Resaca de la Palma in May of 1846. On June 29 Taylor made him aide-de-camp. On August 18, he was promoted to first lieutenant in the Fourth Artillery. For gallant conduct in the battle of Monterrey and the battle of Buena Vista, he was successively breveted captain and major.

His appointment as aide-de-camp to General Taylor expiring on the President-elect's resignation from the Army, Garnett obtained transfer to the Second Regiment of Infantry. When Taylor set out from Baton Rouge, Louisiana, on January 30, 1849, to be sworn in as President, Garnett accompanied him to the national capital. That spring, bearing dispatches to Gen. Persifor F. Smith, military governor of California, at San Francisco, Garnett traveled in company with Congressman T. Butler King of Georgia, confidential agent of President Taylor, who was desirous of speeding the former Mexican territory's organization as a state and its admittance to the Union.

Brevet Major Garnett's signal contribution to the statehood proceedings was his designing of the Great Seal of California.* His sketch, selected from eight or ten that were presented to the constitutional convention at Monterey, was described as "a most happy one." It was adopted with few changes by the convention.

In 1850, under orders from the secretary of war, Garnett conducted a party of 97 migrating Seminoles from Florida to Indian Territory and also a party of 17 of those dispossessed people to Fort Smith, Arkansas, with his customary efficiency.

In 1851 he was a member of a board convened in Washington to devise a new dress uniform and was briefly in command at Corpus Christi. At his next station, Ringgold Barracks, Rio Grande, Texas, he was arrested, January 3, 1852, by order of Brig. Gen. William S. Harney, having declined "to obey his orders to seize the arms and ammunition of certain Americans about 60 miles distant from Ringgold Barracks, who were supposed to be followers of the Mexican insurgent Carbajal," Garnett wrote in summarizing his military record.

Before a 13-member general court Garnett said he had not been properly informed that the arms seizure was to be made under the authority given to the President by the Act of April 20, 1818, prohibiting United States citizens from entering into conspiracies with foreigners. He contended that the order called for what appeared to be commission of an illegal act. He was acquitted, his "position in pronouncing General Harney's order illegal thus fully sustained," he told. The War Department felt otherwise and published a general order informing all officers that orders under the Act of 1818 were legal and should be obeyed. The case attracted wide attention, and Garnett himself published the text of the proceedings.

*In an article relating Garnett's Civil War death to his historical involvement with California, it was noted that he had been placed in charge of a vessel transporting representatives from southern California to the 1849 Constitutional Convention in Monterey. The ship was wrecked on the coast near Point Conception. Subsequently, "while lying in his tent on the sand beach, waiting for relief by another vessel, he [Garnett] conceived the design of our present State Seal." (Sacramento *Daily Union,* August 3, 1861.)

Restored to duty, Garnett continued at Ringgold Barracks until directed to take command of the corps of cadets at West Point, his post from November 1, 1852, to July 31, 1854, under the superintendency of Brevet Col. Robert Edward Lee, an association of future significance. They were old friends. When the major's father was a representative in Congress, he recommended the appointment of young Lee, 18, to the Academy.

Colonel Lee's high regard for his able commandant of cadets could not avail when the latter was summarily removed from duty by Secretary of War Jefferson Davis after Garnett disciplined a cadet for misconduct and advised that he give up the Army as a career. It seemed that the cadet had connections. A letter dated August 23, 1854, at Brighton, England, from "JAS" to Garnett, expressed indignation over the officer's dismissal, indicating it was due to the secretary's displeasure over the disciplining of a relative (allegedly a nephew). JAS said that Garnett should write a letter to the *New York Times* disclosing the situation at the Point, admonishing he never would get ahead unless he forgot his scruples and cultivated friends among the politicians.

Garnett's connection with the Ninth Infantry, with which he would be identified for the remainder of his service in the Army of the United States, started while that regiment was still on paper. Congress, on March 3, 1855, authorized the reactivation of four regiments—the First and Second Cavalry and the Ninth and Tenth Infantry. Garnett immediately applied for promotion to major in one of them. He was transferred to the new First Regiment of Cavalry as senior captain, and was engaged in recruiting, in New York, for its Company A when his appointment as major came through, effective March 27. First he had to deliver 214 cavalry recruits to Jefferson Barracks at St. Louis. That accomplished "without having lost a single man" en route, a singular feat in those times of common desertion, he reported on June 30 at Fortress Monroe as a major of the Ninth.

While recruiting for the cavalry, as Garnett mentioned in career account, he unsuccessfully applied "to be sent East after the camels to be imported to the U.S. for military purposes by the Act of Congress of March 3, 1855." On December 1, 1856, Secretary of War Davis reported to Congress that the experiment of introducing camels—32 of 34 surviving—to southern Texas first for acclimating was proving "as favorable as the most sanguine could have hoped." Tests with camel trains assertedly were satisfactory but on rough ground, out of the sand, the camels got sore-footed, and the sight and smell of them panicked horse and mule outfits. Packers generally disliked the splenetic beasts. The Army continued with them in the Southwest until into the Civil War. Some, in private hands, were used briefly to transport salt in Nevada, and in the 1860s there was a camel freight brigade in British Columbia's Fraser River and Cariboo gold fields.

While on duty in New York and a popular bachelor guest at fashionable functions, the 35-year-old officer met and wooed Miss Marianna Easton Nelson, a belle of the metropolis. Writing from Fortress Monroe on July 20 to his mother at Champlain, he said: "It is proper that I should inform you that I am at length engaged to be married. I should have communicated this intelligence to you sooner perhaps, had it not been only definitively settled a few weeks since. The lady to whom I am engaged is Miss Marianna Easton Nelson of New York. She is an only child. Her father is a Massachusetts gentleman, born at New Bedford, where Miss N. was herself born. Her mother was born at Newport, R.I., and was a Miss Easton. Her parents are both living. She is now 23 years old. Until within the last five years they have lived in Boston. They now reside in N.Y. City in winter, but call themselves Boston people. The young lady is of fair complexion, blue eyes, light hair, slightly under the medium stature, slight of figure, but animate. Her expression of face is considered by all as very pretty and particularly indicative of gentleness and sweetness of disposition. Her mental qualities are good and [she is] very womanly in character, disposition, and [has] most ladylike manners. She is all that I could desire her to be, and eminently suited to my tastes. So much for the woman.

"In position her family are highly respectable, but, like myself, she is poor. This may or may not be a misfortune. I could wish that one of us had been richer but that can't be helped. Had she been rich I suppose she never would have pleased a Garnett for they have a natural affinity for poor people. Her father is, I believe, a stock broker in New York. The time of our marriage is not yet fixed. The movement of my regiment from this place will chiefly control that matter. The probabilities at present however are that we shall marry between the 1st of January and 1st of June next, unless my regiment is sent off sooner. If it is we may not be married for 18 months or perhaps two years to come."

Military matters did intervene and it was not until Garnett could return from his first campaigning in the far Northwest that the vows were taken.

Two newspaper notices brief the story—the romance and tragedy—of the major and Marianna. From the *New York Tribune* of January 24, 1857, under MARRIED:

> Garnett-Nelson—On Tuesday Jan. 22 by the Rev. Dr. Bellows, Major Robert s. Garnett, U.S. Army, to Marianna Easton, only daughter of Geo. T. [*sic*] Nelson of this city.

From the *New York Herald* of December 1, 1858, under DEATHS:

> At Fort Simcoe, Washington Territory, Friday, September 17th, Marianna Eaton [*sic*] in the 27th year of her age, wife of Major Robert S. Garnett, U.S. Army, and daughter of George S. Nelson, Esq. of New York City. Also, at the same place, on the 23rd of the same month, Arthur Nelson, her infant son, aged seven months and five days.
>
> The funeral service will take place at the Church of All Souls, Fourth Avenue and Twenty-first Street, today (Wednesday) at twelve o'clock M whence the remains will be taken to Greenwood. The relatives and friends are invited to attend without further notice.

The records of The Unitarian Church of All Souls, which is now located at Eightieth Street and Lexington Avenue, do not show but it is reasonable to assume that the Rev. Henry Whitney Bellows, whose ministry was from 1839 to 1882, officiated at the funeral services.

On August 28, 1865, the remains of Brigadier General Garnett, CSA, were placed beside those of his wife and son in Green-Wood Cemetery, Brooklyn, near the shaft which he had erected to their memory. In the same plot lie Marianna's parents. The general's body was removed to Green-Wood from the public mausoleum in Greenmount Cemetery, Baltimore, where it had rested since 1861.

(Courtesy Supt. A. R. Koenig, Green-Wood Cemetery.)

JAMES J. ARCHER

James J. Archer (Dec. 19, 1817-Oct. 24, 1874) was born at Stafford, Hartford County, Maryland. He received his formal education at Princeton and at Bacon College, Georgetown, Kentucky, and became a lawyer.

In the Mexican War he was beveted major for gallantry in the storming of Chapultepec, and for his conspicuous service received a vote of thanks from the Maryland legislature. He retired to civil life in 1848 and re-entered the Army as captain in the Ninth Infantry, dating his acceptance of the appointment at Baltimore, March 28, 1855, and giving his age "as between 38 and 39 years."

Following the Army's abandonment of Fort Simcoe, May 22, 1859, Captain Archer commanded the escort for the Northwest Boundary Commission and served in that capacity until the summer of 1861. Before Fort Sumter was fired on, April 12, he had applied for a leave of absence, with the intention of resigning his commission. He sent in his resignation on May 10. But it was not until mid-July, while temporarily at Fort Yamhill, Oregon, that he obtained the impatiently awaited relief from his duties and could say, "I am no longer a U.S. Officer."

Archer relates that he was in command at Fort Yamhill and that he turned over the post to Second Lieut. Phil H. Sheridan, who had been in charge prior to the former's arrival from Fort Colville in northern Washington Territory. However, Sheridan gives a different version:

"In due time orders came for the regiment to go East, and my company went off, leaving me, however—a second lieutenant—in command of the post until I should be relieved by Captain James J. Archer, of the Ninth Infantry, whose company was to take the place of the old garrison. Captain Archer, with his company of the Ninth, arrived shortly after, but I had been notified that he intended to go South, and his conduct was such after reaching the post that I would not turn over the command to him for fear he might commit some rebellious act. Thus a more prolonged detention occurred than I had at first anticipated. Finally the news came that he had tendered his resignation and had been granted a leave of absence for sixty days. On July 17 he took his departure, but I continued in command till September 1, when Captain Philip A. Owen, of the Ninth Infantry, arrived and, taking charge, gave me my release."

Archer's exchange of goodbyes at Fort Vancouver with his late commander, Colonel Wright, and other officers, was felicitous, but Archer gained a wrong impression. "Col. Wright's parting with me," the captain wrote, "was very kind. He expressed real regret at my leaving his regiment but not a word of disapproval. I think he was satisfied I was right although he could not say so." The colonel was true-blue to the Union.

Commissioned a Confederate brigadier on June 3, 1862, Archer took part in all the important engagements of the Army of Northern Virginia in 1862-63. Captured at Gettysburg, he was a prisoner for over a year—at Point Lookout, Maryland, and Johnson's Island, Sandusky Bay, Ohio. Exchanged, he resumed his old command, but his health was shattered. He died October 24, 1874.

JOHN ELLIS WOOL

Commander of the Department of the Pacific during most of Fort Simcoe's Army service, John Ellis Wool was born in Newburgh, New York, February 20, 1784, and died in Troy, that state, November 10, 1869. A monument 75 feet in height was raised to his memory in Troy, with an inscription by William Cullen Bryant: "This stone is erected to Major-General John Ellis Wool, the gallant soldier, the able commander, and the patriotic citizen, distinguished in many battles."

Native of Orange County, Wool joined the volunteer corps at the outbreak of the War of 1812, recruited a company, fought at Queenstown Heights and was promoted major, Twenty-ninth Infantry. For conspicuous service, Plattsburg, September 6, 1814, he was breveted lieutenant colonel, became inspector general of the Army, colonel of cavalry and brigadier general, 1841. As inspector general, Wool traveled horseback over much of the country. In the war with Mexico he commanded a column of volunteer regiments, and joined forces with Gen. Zachary Taylor in defeating Santa Ana at Buena Vista, 1847.

General Wool's service in the Department of the Pacific began with his selection by President Pierce and Secretary of War Davis in December, 1853, to check filibustering expeditions fitting out from California against the territories of Mexico. The United States was engaged in negotiating the Gadsden Purchase for $10,000,000, ultimately a tract of 29,640 square miles south of the Gila River and from the Rio Grande to the Colorado River. Violations of Mexican soil could jeopardize the undertaking or cause another war, which the President sought to avoid. Wool acted expeditiously to secure arrests for violation of the neutrality laws of the United States.

Indian troubles on the Pacific Coast were also his concern. From headquarters at San Francisco in February, 1855, Wool reported that there had been fighting between a small party of whites seeking to exterminate Indians on Salmon River and another party of whites trying to protect the Indians. Difficulties on immigrant travel routes to the West and in mining areas accelerated. Wool developed definite and publicly-expressed views on leaving the "Indian Country" to the Indians which involved him in controversy over more than military problems. When he asked to be relieved of his command at Benicia (an event welcome to political authorities in the Pacific Northwest) and assigned to the Eastern Department on December 4, 1856, he observed that the Western Department was well-organized for protection of white inhabitants and control of Indians.

In 1860 General Wool took charge of the Department of the East and at the opening of the Civil War saved Fortress Monroe by timely reinforcement, and afterward commanded there as head of the Department of Virginia. He was promoted a major general. May 16, 1862, and retired August 1, 1863.

GEORGE WRIGHT

Selecting the site for Fort Simcoe was a responsibility of Vermont's George Wright, born in the village of Norwich on the Connecticut River, October 21, 1803. He entered the U.S. Military Academy at the age of 14 years, 11 months and was twenty-fourth in the class of 40 graduates, 1822.

Of frontiers awaiting, his last was the farthest west. First duty for the second lieutenant, Third Infantry, was at Fort Howard, Wisconsin, 1822-24. At Fort Leavenworth, new post on the Missouri in unorganized Kansas Territory, he was commissioned first lieutenant, September 23, 1827. Captain, 1836, he served on the northern frontier during the Canada border disturbances. He was transferred to the Eighth Infantry, July 7, 1838, and in the war against the Florida Indians, 1840-42, won brevet to major for "meritorious conduct, zeal, energy, perseverance." In the war with Mexico he was breveted twice for "gallant and meritorious conduct"—to lieutenant colonel, to colonel, earned commanding a storming party at Molino del Rey, where he was wounded.

While in garrison at Fort Ontario, New York, he was promoted major, January 1, 1848. From Fort Columbus, New York, he was sent to take charge of the Northern District of California, headquarters Fort Reading, September 17, 1852-May 19, 1855, and was advanced there to lieutenant colonel. March 3, 1855, he was commissioned colonel, Ninth Infantry, and took command of the regiment at Fort Monroe.

Commanding the Northern District (Columbia River and Puget Sound) of the Department of the Pacific, 1856-1858, he led the decisive Spokane expedition that closed the Yakima War. His headquarters was Fort Dalles, 1856-59, and he was on frontier duty at Fort Walla Walla, 1859-60. From July 5, 1860, to September 13, 1861, he directed the Department of Oregon. Brigadier general, U.S. Volunteers, September 28, 1861, he commanded the Department of the Pacific from October 20, 1861, to July 1, 1864, and the District of California to July 27, 1865. "For long, faithful, and meritorious services," he was breveted brigadier general, December 19, 1864.

To head the new Department of the Columbia, headquarters Fort Vancouver, he sailed with staff and Mrs. Wright at noon, July 28, 1865, from San Francisco on the overloaded sidewheeler *Brother Jonathan* into a gale outside the Golden Gate. In the continuing storm the vessel struck a submerged rock July 30 at 2 p.m., about eight miles off Crescent City, and sank with most of the 240 persons aboard. A few escaped in small boats.

Many bodies were found southward along the coast, the general's at Bay Flat near Shelter Cove, Mendocino County, 150 miles from the scene of the disaster, the *Alta California* reported on October 13. Mrs. Wright's remains were recovered earlier. The general's horse and one of two pack camels were washed ashore.

Services for the Wrights were held Saturday, October 21, in San Francisco, and the next day in Sacramento, where the remains were conveyed by steamer with an honor guard of officers and Ninth Infantry sergeants. The coffins were displayed on a catafalque in the senate chamber of the capitol until escorted to the Eighth Street Congregational Church for services by three ministers.

The *Sacramento Daily Union* reported that church bells and fire bells tolled, "all flags of the city were displayed at half-mast and trimmed with emblems of mourning," and the front of the New Orleans Hotel, "formerly the home of General Wright, was festooned with drapery." The general's hearse was drawn by six black horses, the hearse of Mrs. Wright by four grays. The cortege, over a mile in length, "was the largest ever witnessed in this city."

Interment was in one grave in the City Cemetery Legislative Plot (Center run A-52 Lot 42, as now designated)*. The Rev.

*In the same plot, but not noted on the 20-foot shaft, lies the first son of George and Margaret Forster Wright—Col. Thomas Forster Wright, killed in the Modoc War, April 26, 1873, aged 43 years. The colonelcy dated to a

Dudley Chase, chaplain, U.S.A., stationed at Benicia, read the Episcopal Church service, attended by all the city's clergy, and "just as the setting sun was dropping behind the Coast Range," said the *Daily Bee,* "a battalion of the Fourth fired the salute of three volleys."

WILLIAM KOHLHAUFF

Sgt. William Kohlhauff, credited with finding the spot chosen for Fort Simcoe, was born in St. Albans, Bavaria, October 21, 1828, immigrated to the United States in 1849, and enlisted on August 31 that year, in Company A, Sixth Infantry. He served five years at Forts Ripley and Snelling, Minnesota Territory. Honorably discharged at the expiration of his term of service, August 31, 1854, he went to St. Louis. There, February 20, 1855, he married Johanna Saling, whose family lived near his in Bavaria.

In May, 1855, he enlisted at Jefferson Barracks, Missouri, in the Ninth Infantry, and was assigned to Company B, with which he and Mrs. Kohlhauff went to Washington Territory, in Colonel Wright's command. At expiration of his enlistment in May, 1860, he reportedly built the first house of boards in Walla Walla and engaged in a general merchandise business with another ex-sergeant of his company, and in 1862 built a better residence, where his children (15, it is said) were reared. In Walla Walla he was a member of the school board and city council.

On May 1, 1883, the family removed to Spokane, where he was in the mercantile business and on the city council. Mrs. Kohlhauff died on December 21, 1905, and Mr. Kohlhauff on April 29, 1907. They were buried at Fairmount Cemetery, from St. Aloysius Church. His grave is marked with a Quartermaster Department tombstone telling his rank and connection with the Ninth Infantry.

---

period of Volunteer service. His regular rank was first lieutenant of infantry. There too is Montgomery Michaux Owen, grandson of the George Wrights, and son of Capt. and Mrs. Philip A. Owen, who was buried on September 20, 1866. Born in Washington Territory, he died December 20, 1861, at the age of two years, three months, in San Francisco, and first was buried in that city's Lone Mountain Cemetery. He is identified beneath the inscription for the Wrights simply as M. M. Owen.

LOUIS SCHOLL

Louis Scholl, architect of Simcoe, German emigrant of 1848, was a remarkable westerner and one of the Army's almost indispensable men. With a precise and facile pen, an affinity for figures, a knack for sketching and a bobtailed education, he was just the cultivated young gentleman the Army needed in the frontier West of the 1850s. Already, at adventurous 25, he was a saddle-tough veteran of the Oregon Trail when he struck up with the Army in Great Salt Lake City in the waning summer of 1854. Recognizing talents rare in time and place, the Army presently put him to work. He could turn a hand, it seemed, to almost anything. Clerk, draftsman, topographer, guide, scout, packer, wagonmaster, he proved a valuable adjunct in camp, garrison or on the road, from Utah Territory to the State of California and in the Territories of Oregon and Washington. In the early throes of the Civil War he ably assisted McClellan's Army of the Potomac and was otherwise useful to the national cause. Again in 1877, when the Wallowa Valley's galled Nez Perces went out, he helped the troops, and in last association wore for the first time the uniform.

Fort Simcoe is something of a memorial to Louis Scholl. The pleasing lines and proportions of the post-Colonial style quarters—the deep, pillared verandas, shuttered front porch windows reaching to the floor in the captains' residences, interior moldings—all attest Scholl's skill and artistry. For three years—1856-59—clerk and draftsman for Capt. Thomas Jordan, assistant quartermaster at Fort Dalles—Scholl contributed to the building of Fort Simcoe, to contemporaneous construction of the new Fort Dalles and Fort Walla Walla, and in the building of Fort Colville—now long gone.

Louis Scholl, born November 4, 1829, in Karlsruhe, had a family tree tracing to 1487. He was the fourth son in ten children. His father, Carl Friedrich Scholl, was president of the Staats Amortisations Bank. Schooling at the Karlsruhe Polytechnic was terminated on the collapse of the republican revolution of 1848. There were many student and other hasty departures. Of the Scholl brothers, eldest Carl fled to Switzerland, taught at the University of Berne. Louis, Emil, Julius and Ernst skipped to America, and later came another brother and two sisters. Emil and Julius, in the Civil War, wore the gray; the former was wounded, the latter died, 1862, in a Richmond hospital.

In New York two years, piano-playing tenor Louis worked for a music house. He visited the South, tried farming at St. Charles, Missouri, where Ernst died, 1850, and drove an ox team to California in 1852, a "cholera Year," but the train was ahead of the disease. He sketched "some of the important objects," Chimney Rock, Court House Rock, Platte Bluffs, Forts Kearney and Laramie, Independence Rock, the Humboldt Mountains, and flunked a buffalo hunt. "Twelve of the sketches made at this time earned me my first money in the New Eldorado, being published in the Christmas number of the Sacramento 'Union', and bringing me a check for forty-eight dollars." ("Recollections of Sixty Years.")

With a speculation in livestock, he started for Salt Lake City in the spring of 1853 and while encamped in Thousand Spring Valley near Goose Creek at the head of Humboldt River lost some of his horses to rustlers. By passing express rider he sent word of the thievery to Salt Lake, returned to California, and in the *Union* of February 21, 1854, read of the arrest of the thieves and sentencing of one to the penitentiary. Renewing his enterprise, he left in the spring with the hope of recovering his property. He saw Salt Lake Mayor J. C. Little riding one of the stolen horses and had "interesting interviews with Justice Smith, editor of the *Deseret News,* and Gov. Brigham Young," but had to be content with the information that proceeds of a sheriff's sale of the animals were "appropriated for the 'perpetual emigration fund.'"

Scholl found bivouacked for two days on the public square Brevet Lieut. Col. Edward Jevnor Steptoe, Third Artillery, just arrived—August 31—from Fort Leavenworth, Kansas Territory, with recruits and remounts for posts in Oregon and California. The expedition—92 days, 64 marching days, 1,216 miles out of Leavenworth—consisted of two artillery companies, 85 dragoon recruits and quartermaster train under Capt. Rufus Ingalls, who had 130 citizen employes—teamsters, hostlers and herders—for 450 mules, 300 horses, 70 heavy baggage wagons and seven light wagons. The total complement was 300 soldiers and civilians and nine officers. Six mules drew each heavy wagon. To each of the seven light wagons were attached the replacement horses, two abreast, in convenient sections, managed by a rider of the near leader and by the driver of the wagon, and always led at a walk. In that fashion the captain got his remounts through day by day without loss, and at night staked and under guard.

Friendships formed with Steptoe and Ingalls shaped Scholl's course the next decade. He was employed as court clerk by the new Utah territorial chief justice, John F. Kinney, who, with the new attorney general, had traveled under Steptoe's protection. The colonel had assured that in event he accepted presidential appointment as governor to succeed Brigham Young, Scholl would be his private secretary. The appointment by Franklin Pierce arrived on December 24. Steptoe deliberated 48 hours and declined the honor, "not desiring," said Scholl, "to give up his military career and mix with politics." Nor would it have been politic, such was Governor Young's standing with the people of Utah. Then a memorial signed by Steptoe, his officers, the federal officials and prominent citizens, for reappointment of Young as governor and as superintendent of Indian affairs was sent to the President, who granted the request.

"In January 1855," Scholl wrote, "I accepted a position as commissary clerk under Capt. Rufus Ingalls—the quartermaster of Col. Steptoe's expedition, at the same time making a map of the country from Salt Lake Valley to California and Fort Lane, Oregon, giving distances from watercourses to next camp."

Incidental to the march west was an errand to secure, if practicable, the slayers of Capt. John W. Gunnison and seven of his topographical survey party, massacred at breakfast, October 25, 1853, near Sevier Lake, a hundred miles south of Great Salt Lake, Of eight Indians finally brought to trial with the influence of Governor Young, three were convicted by a jury, but merely for manslaughter. By connivance or carelessness, they soon mysteriously escaped.

But for the Indian-catching assignment, the march could have been completed that season. Arrangements had to be made for a winter layover. Forty-five miles south of Salt Lake City a grazing camp was established in uninhabited Rush Valley and the employes kept busy "day and night," Captain Ingalls reported, cutting and hauling some 200 tons of hay and 300 cords of wood, tending the mules and horses, erecting quarters, stables, a storehouse and corrals. For his command, Steptoe rented quarters in the city. The dragoon recruits frequently rode south into Indian country, clanking the sabre and getting a whiff of buckskin.

Scholl wrote: "Col. Steptoe occupied a plainly furnished room near the public square. Chief Justice Kinney and family occupied, with the sutler's store, the first story of a two-story adobe building. Attorney General Holman roomed with clerks in the big upstairs hall and there was mirth and song every night. A melodeon at which I presided was the musical instrument. Often the officers had dances when some of the Mormon ladies were surreptitiously taken to the gatherings without the knowledge of parents. Some good performances were given at the beautiful theater and there the sisters Guggenheim were the stars." Robert O. Tyler, second lieutenant, Third Artillery, nephew of John Tyler, tenth President, "was wit and life and musical light of many pleasant evenings." Seven years later Scholl stood near Brigadier General Tyler on Rappahannock Heights when the latter opened his siege gun cannonade at Fredericksburg.

The expense of wintering the expedition in Salt Lake Basin, Captain Ingalls reported to the quartermaster general, totaled $208,449.58, "quite heavy" he considered, and owing in part to foraging the animals with grain and hay during a severe period.

On resumption of the march in April, newly promoted 1st Lieut. Sylvester Mowry, Third Artillery, was detached with recruits and horses to proceed by way of the new Mormon settlement of Las Vegas to Fort Tejon, southern California. Steptoe, closely followed by Ingalls, marched north from the city for 60 miles through settled country to Bear River, around the head of the lake to the Humboldt, reached May 28, to Lassen (Humboldt) Meadows, June 10. There the commands separated. The colonel, with the artillery companies, took the old Carson Valley route, arriving July 12 at Benicia. The captain turned west for stockaded Fort Lane in southern Oregon with his civilians, Allston's 50 dragoons, mules, wagons and remounts, "fine bay horses," appraised expert Scholl.

Lieut. Benjamin Allston, Academy '53, traveled in high style, having, said Scholl, "a fine conveyance with coal black horses and a negro coachman all the way from the Missouri River."

The lieutenant resigned, June 20, 1857, at Benicia and returned home to be a rice planter and aide-de-camp, with rank of lieutenant colonel, to his father, South Carolina's Gov. Robert F. W. Allston, a West Point graduate of 1821, and joined in the Rebellion in '61.

On a bright July 6 Ingalls unsaddled and unhitched at Fort Lane in the Rogue River Valley, where reapers were in the fields of wheat, pleasing picture at the end of a long trail, 368 miles from the meadows left on June 14. Nothing, Ingalls said in his official report to Thomas S. Jesup, quartermaster general, was lost or abandoned, and all the animals made it nicely. The early stretch included a 40-mile traverse of Black Rock Desert, marked by "sadly frequent" signs of a migration in the late, or hot, season of 1852—burnt and whole wagons, bleached bones of oxen and "all manner of property usually seen in immigrant trains." "I almost wished myself back with Col. Steptoe," he said. After the desert, grass and water were always abundant—a more charming country he'd never seen—and the animals improved each day. Progress was facilitated by keeping an advance party to remove obstacles.

The main ridge of the Sierras was crossed on 23rd June and the column descended to "lovely" Goose Lake, in the vicinity of "Clear (Am-pa) Rhett's and Klamath lakes," and the Cascades were crossed "through Applegate's Pass, or on a trace cleared by him some years ago," Ingalls reported.

The 122 horses and 112 mules, delivered "in fine condition," were a welcome sight to Capt. Andrew J. Smith and his First Dragoons, crippled for transportation in the Rogue River War, and the wagons, Ingalls added, "very acceptable at Forts Lane and Scott, as cannot be got there from any other direction without great expense and difficulty." After three days at Fort Lane, Ingalls took all the animals not needed there to Fort Reading, northern California, and hurried on to Benicia to pay off and discharge the civilian employes with Steptoe's expedition. Guiding the civilians of Ingalls' train, Scholl followed to department headquarters. There, he said, "I prepared the official map of the expedition from Salt Lake for Colonel Steptoe and Captain and Quartermaster Ingalls."

Fort Dalles, Scholl's place of employment, 1856-59, began as Camp Drum, established in 1850 by a detachment of the

Left is parlor fireplace, Fort Simcoe CO's quarters, before restoration. (H. D. Guie photo.) Below is restored marble-painted wooden facing and mantle. Diningroom fireplace was similarly treated. (Gladys Seufert photo, 1969, OHS Collections.)

Mounted Rifles from Columbia Barracks (by 1853 Fort Vancouver) and named for Capt. Simon Henry Drum, killed in the assault on Mexico City, 1847. In 1851 it was garrisoned by a First Artillery detachment, succeeded in May, 1852, by K Company, Fourth Infantry, Brevet Maj. Benjamin Alvord. Under him the post became Fort Dalles, in 1853, identifying with the neighboring riverside settlement of Dalles, soon to be The Dalles, the postal name as of 1860. First applied by French-Canadian river runners of the fur trade era, *dalles* described an extensive basaltic chute terminating just upstream.

With Capt. Thomas Jordan, lately quartermaster at Fort Miller on the San Joaquin, central California, Scholl reached Fort Dalles in early March, 1856. Theirs was an eventful January trip on the Pacific Mail's SS *Republic* from San Francisco to Fort Vancouver. Stormy seas ignited a deck cargo of lime—120 barrels were jettisoned. At a call of "fire" the next day, half of 20 tons of Army gunpowder stowed below went overside. In the haven of Port Orford the fire was controlled. Through the gale and fires the female passengers, including Mrs. Capt. Frederick T. Dent, Company B, Ninth Infantry, and female servant, were confined to the afterdeck cabin, in a clutter of blankets, provisions and kegs of water, while officers and Scholl guarded the two swinging lifeboats.

"I see yet Capt. Jordan toiling up the steps with a 100-pound barrel of gunpowder on his shoulder," Scholl recalled. "I rolled them overboard, continuing my vigil over the lifeboat."

Fort Dalles hiring reports show Scholl listed successively as storehouse keeper and assisting with plans for storehouse and quarters, as supervising and laying out building construction, and lastly, in July, 1858, as forage master. In his own words, he was "employed as clerk and draftsman" by Captain Jordan, "and for three years following acted as supervising architect of the government, making all the plans for Fort Dalles, also for Fort Walla Walla, Fort Simcoe and Colville."

Also in his "Recollections of Sixty Years" he wrote: "All doors, window sashes, mantels, bookcases, etc. for these far posts were transported, some by pack mule but mostly by large six-mule wagon trains. Charles Russel's, the wagonmaster's 24-mule teams were for two years constantly employed towards Walla Walla and a pack train of nearly 50 mules moved between

Villa Farm House, Design XX, from Downing's *Architecture of Country Houses,* was inspiration for Ft. Simcoe CO's quarters design, almost identical.

Fort Dalles and Simcoe. . . . I prepared all working plans for the 49 carpenters and masons." Elsewhere he noted: "All exterior and interior finished articles were made by hand planing at the Post at Dalles. Doors, sashes, mantelpieces, writing desks, bookcases, wardrobe & bedsteads for Officers Qrs were all made and designed at Post and working plans also sent up to Walla Walla & Simcoe."

For their building projects Scholl and Jordan had professional guidance—texts and pictures published by Andrew Jackson Downing (1815-52) of Newburgh, New York, successful nurseryman and landscape gardener who turned to architecture. Not a finished draftsman, he depended to large extent on architects of some note to whip into shape his designs for what he advocated as tasteful American homes. Period and regional borrowings were incorporated with his own interesting and practical ideas. His *Cottage Residences,* 1842, went through four editions. His *Architecture of Country Houses,* published in 1850

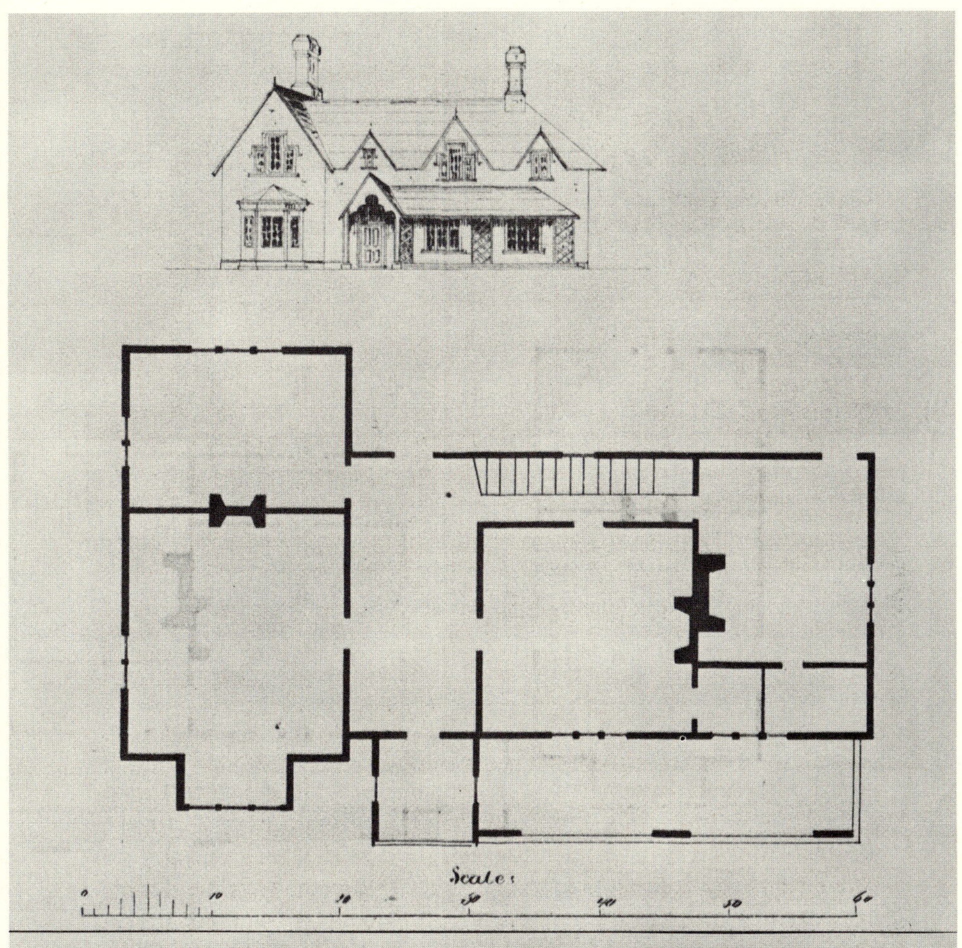

Louis Scholl's drawing of Fort Simcoe CO's quarters. (National Archives, RG 92, Consolidated Correspondence File, Fort Dalles.)

and of which there were nine editions by 1866, provided all the information that the Army's architect from Baden required.

Forts Simcoe and Walla Walla were laid out rectangularly—Simcoe as a square. Fort Dalles, fitted octagonally to its hilly site, was architecturally unique in the realm of western posts. Quarters for commandant and officers at Fort Dalles were em-

Fort Simcoe, rear of CO's quarters.

bellished strikingly in Downing style, with bays and oriels, pretty porches and decorative chimney tops, scrolled trim, hooded and bracketed windows. Last of the Fort Dalles structures, the well-preserved residence for the medical officer, hints at the distinctive treatment of regimental headquarters. Simpler Fort Simcoe and plainer Fort Walla Walla no less adorned their settings.

An important feature of the frame quarters for officers at the three posts was the brick nogging for insulation—one course brick between the studding, to fill the whole frame. Some partitions were similarly reinforced. Downing called it "filling in" and "the best mode of making such wooden houses comfortable and warm." Dobies the bricks were called by some, by others salmon brick—sun dried or kiln baked as at Simcoe.

Commandant and captains quarters at Fort Simcoe suggest adaptation of American colonial and rural Dixie. The post commander's two-story, sharply gabled residence closely resembles "A Villa Farm-House in the Bracketed Style" in Downing's *Architecture of Country Houses.* Out of the book are many features, interior and exterior, including the mullioned parlor bay close to the Gothic-like facaded entry, the long and wide veranda with trellis posts, and the grouping of narrow, diamond-paned windows upstairs and down. Board-and-batten plank siding furthers a favorite Downing motif—"the perpendicular."

The story-and-a-half captain's quarters—three front-in-line with the commandant's—also board-and-battened, with deep verandas and a pair, each, of tall porch windows shuttered to the floor, lend a feeling of Old South. As per Downing, too, the hewn, pine-log wall quarters for subalterns and enlisted men had the useful luxury of long verandas.

Sills for the quarters and other structures were squared, interlocking pine timbers on blocks of dressed stone. The shingles, locally "shakes," were shaved in a forest gorge four miles west of the post. Fireplace stone was quarried at The Dalles. Fireplaces and chimneys in the interior walls assured better draught and more heat. Walls and ceilings were finished with plaster or ten-inch boards, painted. Flooring was random-width pine.

Woodwork and shutter blinds were stained and grained in imitation of oak—a Downing treatment of "plain woods."

Washed with a solution of sulphuric acid—an ounce to a pint of warm water—the wood was rubbed lightly with tobacco stain and when dry was brushed with a mixture of one-half pound of beeswax, one-half pint of linseed oil and one pint of boiled linseed oil. Optionally it then was varnished and polished. The technique guided Albert Culverwell, parks commission historian, and Ernest Norling, Seattle artist, in restoring woodwork in the commandant's house to its original texture in 1956. They also renovated the mantels and facings of the parlor and dining room fireplaces to resemble marble.

Removal of a screened back porch, as a part of the restoration, disclosed the original brick terrace between the kitchen wing and the bathroom wing. In the corridor to the kitchen is a sealed small door that once opened on a stair to a basement storage room, filled with earth when found frequented by some of the rattlesnakes abounding in the vicinity.

The main hall stairway, railed with handsomely turned alder wood from The Dalles, rises at the back wall to a landing and reverses to the second story. The central room was the commanding officer's business office, adjoined by the adjutant's office and quarters and giving a view east to the parade and over the Toppenish plain. Two of the "attick" rooms, as Garnett called them, were bedrooms for visiting officers. A closed stairway from a ground level entrance on the north side of the building afforded use of the second floor without disturbing domestic occupancy below.

While on the quartermaster's payroll at Fort Dalles Scholl made a survey in 1858 of Fort Vancouver for General Harney, commanding the Department of the Columbia. In April of the following year the general assigned him to find and map a new overland route from The Dalles to the Salt Lake Valley, with a company of the Fourth Infantry. On that expedition he named Harney Valley after the general and Jordan Valley after his good friend, the captain, who, incidentally, in 1861 would join the Confederacy and become chief of staff to Gen. Pierre Gustave Toutant de Beauregard.

In the spring of 1860 Scholl left Fort Dalles to guide Capt. A. J. Smith's command through Harney Valley. Attacked by Indians in the Owyhee country, Smith retired to the Harney meadows to await Maj. Enoch Steen, who was exploring for a route across the Cascades near the head of Deschutes River.

Scholl volunteered to locate and hurry Major Steen and to continue for additional help to Fort Vancouver. Accompanied by Cayuse George (George Rundel of Tygh Valley) and each leading a spare horse, Scholl covered the 380 miles to Vancouver—including the 90 miles down the Columbia by steamer from The Dalles—in three nights and two days.

"The summer of 1861," Scholl tells in an application for a pension (which was never granted because of his civilian capacity), "I passed at Fort Walla Walla, the guest of Maj. Steen, and in the autumn of same year a military expedition was to be sent to Mazatlan over Mexican territory to relieve Fort Worth, Texas, 600 mules and wagons having been gathered at Fort Walla Walla. They were sent to Fort Vancouver under Col. Wright's son, George Wright, he taking the first 300 head and wagons, and I followed with the remainder, being 300 head and some wagons. He transported his animals and wagons by Capt. Dall's steamer to Benicia at the heavy expense of over $20,000, but I chose the land route, arriving at Benicia with all animals in fine order at only $3,500 expense to the government; his first arrivals in a sorry plight from severe chafing on board of vessel. I arrived in November at Benicia, but the expedition did not take place, the Union troops having surrendered with an enormous quantity of military stores at Fort Worth to the rebel government."

In Washington, D.C., during January and February of 1862, Scholl acted as private secretary for Sen. James W. Nesmith of Oregon, "preparing mostly the transfer of several hundred thousand dollars worth of Indian war bonds to the proper owners in Oregon." On February 28 he accepted a clerkship again under Captain Ingalls (soon promoted to lieutenant colonel) to handle transportation details. He immediately was put to work receiving, at Annapolis Naval Station, the immense fleet of vessels engaged by the War Department to take McClellan's Army to Urbana, Virginia. Shortly thereafter he was assistant harbormaster at Fortress Monroe, and, as the expedition moved south, he handled complex phases of sea and land transport, took wagon trains to the front, and was at various times under fire. On several occasions he applied for a commission in the Third Artillery, having been with and near that organization on the Pacific Coast. "But," he says, "the invariable answer of Col. Ingalls, 'Louis, I can't spare you,' silenced me."

When President Lincoln, in November of 1862, sent Gen.

Ambrose E. Burnside to relieve McClellan of his command, Scholl played a part in that drama. From McClellan's office tent near Warrenton, at 1:30 o'clock in the morning, Scholl started with dispatches that included "Little Mac's" resignation. The countersign, not inappropriately, was "Waterloo." By horse to Gen. Carl Schurz's headquarters near Centerville and thence to Alexandria, Scholl finished his trip by tug to Washington, where, he relates, "I delivered my dispatches and laid them on the Secretary of War's table, he being absent at lunch."

Present at the taking of Fredericksburg and at its evacuation, Scholl contracted pneumonia and rheumatism that dark December, and gave up his work for a position as draughtsman with the capital buildings architect in Washington. He spent many weeks gathering information on hospital needs and drawing hospital plans.

For his health, Scholl returned west in September, 1863, to The Dalles. On February 18, 1864, he married Miss Elizabeth Fulton, of a pioneer Oregon family. They had three sons, Carl, Louis Jr. and Bismarck. A daughter died in infancy.

At Boise City, Idaho, 1870, Scholl was draftsman and supervising assistant for construction of the U.S. Assay Office. In 1874-75 he compiled the sessions laws of the Idaho Territorial Legislature, sharpening his own goose quill pens, which he preferred to steel pens. Civilian quartermaster clerk at Fort Boise, 1877, he fitted out a pack train for Col. E. V. Sumner, reinforcing Maj. Gen. Oliver O. Howard's pursuit of the Nez Perces through the Bitterroots. On the command's return, Scholl accompanied it to the Presidio, San Francisco, to help Lieut. Robert Fletcher prepare the official map of the campaign. On November 6, 1877, Scholl enlisted for five years—a private in the Topographical Assistant Detachment, the Engineer Office, Headquarters, Military Division of the Pacific and Department of California—pay and emoluments $95 a month. The enlistment was terminated April 30, 1879, under Special Orders No. 44, due, said Scholl, to illness—pneumonia, rheumatism, bad eyesight.

Lt. Col. J. C. Kelton, A.A.G., commanding, described Scholl as 49½ years of age, 5 feet, 11¾ inches tall, of dark complexion, with gray eyes and brown hair. Carl F. Palfrey, first lieutenant, Engineers, wrote the character reference: "Excellent. A skilled draughtsman, especially in topographical work, and a faithful employe.''

Retiring to Walla Walla, Scholl was employed as bookkeeper by his brother-in-law, H. P. Isaacs, operating the Pacific Flour Mills Company, a family enterprise for which Scholl once worked at Boise. For the same company he designed a mill at Prescott, Washington, and was plant superintendent. Also, he and his family developed a homestead near Ritzville, in Adams County, and for six years he and his three sons had Scholl Bros. flour mill at Walla Walla.

In Los Angeles, where he and Mrs. Scholl were sojourning, Scholl died on June 4, 1911, aged 82 years. Mrs. Scholl died in Walla Walla, February 5, 1915. They were buried in Wasco Cemetery at The Dalles.

GRANVILLE OWEN HALLER

Granville Owen Haller, who opened for the Army at the Toppenish crossing, and had it nip-and-tuck there with the Yakimas, wasn't raised to be a soldier. His mother, who had his rearing from the age of two, wanted him to study for the ministry but he aspired to a military career, as a West Pointer, no less. Born January 21, 1819, in York, Pennsylvania, he was the son of George and Susan (Pennington) Haller, natives of the locality. The father died in 1821.

Turning 20, Granville applied for a cadetship at the Academy, and was asked to appear before a board convened in the City of Washington, passed its examination and ''received from President Martin Van Buren, through the Hon. Joel R. Poinsett, secretary of war,'' he tells in his *Memoir of Military Services,* a second lieutenancy in the Fourth Infantry, 17 November 1839.

He early learned about Indians, joining his regiment, 1840, at Fort Gibson, ''a very sickly post in the Cherokee Nation of Indians,'' and then in the Florida War against the Seminoles. He participated in all the battles in the Valley of Mexico and was in the storming party at Molino del Rey. In Brevet Col. John Garland's report of the capture of the City of Mexico appears: ''I must not omit to call attention of the General to Lieut. Haller, of the 4th Inf., who gave 'evidence of courage and good conduct; his efforts were untiring and crowned with good results; and also to Lieut. Grant, of the same regiment.' " From Maj. Francis Lee's report: "Haller and 2nd Lieutenants Grant and Judah behaved with distinguished gallantry on the 13th and 14th." For his services in Mexico, Haller was twice breveted —to captain and to major, in September, 1847.

On June 21, 1849, he married Henrietta M. Cox, also of York, Pennsylvania.

Service on the Pacific Slope began in 1852 with a seven months voyage around the Horn to San Francisco—on the U.S. Storeship *Fredonia*—and thence by steamer to Fort Vancouver. In July, 1853, he took station at Fort Dalles, "a dreary and isolated spot," said he, and the next year was after Indians again. Following the 1856 Yakima Indian campaign, he constructed a timber post, Fort Townsend, near new Port Townsend at the entrance to Puget Sound. His company's task of clearing the dense forest of towering firs three to six feet in diameter and grading the slope overlooking the salt water was "severe and immense," he wrote, and he had to guard against desertions to the Fraser River gold diggings in British Columbia. In August, 1859, he took his company to Fort Mojave, "regarded as the very worst post in the United States"—all supplies were hauled 300 miles from San Pedro, California. Mojave was evacuated in 1861 and the garrison marched 400 miles to embark at San Diego for New York. In Washington City, December 19, Haller was promoted major. He was in the Virginia and Maryland campaigns, and at York, his birthplace, recruited volunteers, and just before Gettysburg took part in efforts to check Jubal Early's advance in Pennsylvania.

A hot punch party in his tent on Rappahannock, opposite Fredericksburg, December 17, 1862, put Haller out of the Army. An allegedly fuddled Navy friend and visitor, Lieut. Comdr. Clark H. Wells, felt obliged to report to Secretary of War Stanton that Haller offered a toast expressing disloyal sentiments: "Here's to a northern confederacy and a southern one while Lincoln is President." Further, Wells complained—by letter and in person—Haller had blamed the administration for military mistakes and declared General McClellan should have been left in command of the Army. Wells also wrote to Haller, lecturing him and advising of the report to Stanton.

Actually, Haller protested, his toast, offered to a fellow

major, was: "The Constitution as it is, the Union as it was." He gathered testimonials as to his loyalty, asked for a hearing, and was ignored. On July 25, 1863, he was dismissed the service "for disloyal conduct and the utterance of disloyal sentiments" (Special Orders No. 331). In vain appeal to Stanton for a court of inquiry, Haller said that Wells, whom he had known for a long time, was crazy and only lately released from a lunatic asylum.

Sixteen years later, March 3, 1879, a joint resolution of Congress granted a court of inquiry, which held that Haller had been wrongfully dismissed. President Rutherford B. Hayes, distinguished veteran of the Civil War, approved the findings. Haller was commissioned a colonel of infantry, to rank from February 19, 1873, at which date he would have received a colonelcy in a normal course of service, and was assigned to the Twenty-third Infantry.

The year after dismissal by the Army, Haller returned with his family to Puget Sound, to Whidbey Island, farmed and ran a general store. He developed real estate, particularly farm properties in several Sound localities, and for 14 years was a leading resident of Seattle, where he died, May 2, 1897, survived by Mrs. Haller, one of two sons and one of two daughters.

An oldest contemporary lately recalled that the Hallers were The First Family on Seattle's fashionable First Hill.

ANTHONY (ANTON) HEGER

Anthony (Anton) Heger was born in Vienna, Austria, December 4, 1828. His father, Anton Heger, M.D., who was head of the Allgemeine Spital (General Hospital) in Vienna, traveled to the United States in 1843 to study yellow fever and other diseases, and in 1847 published a book giving an account of his trip to America. Subsequently he returned to this country to study smallpox among the Indians, fell ill and died in Sacramento, California.

Young Anthony, who studied medicine in Vienna, was so impressed by his father's description of America that he came over in 1848. In 1850 he returned to the family home to get his sisters, Theresa and Frances. The sisters settled in Philadelphia, and Dr. Heger opened an office in Pottsville, Pennsylvania, with a Dr. Halberstadt, as a general practitioner.

On August 29, 1856, he accepted a captaincy in the Medical Corps, and on September 30 he married Miss Anna Margaret Whitney, of Pottsville, born November 27, 1828, in Philadelphia. Shortly after the marriage they took passage to San Francisco, on their way to Simcoe.

Dr. Heger later was medical director of Hammond Hospital at Point Lookout, Maryland, where the North's largest prison was established August 1, 1863. There Mrs. Heger died on September 28, 1864. On March 13, 1865, Dr. Heger was breveted lieutenant colonel for faithful and meritorious service. He attained the grade of colonel and surgeon on January 2, 1891, was retired at the age of 64 years on December 4, 1892, and advanced to the rank of brigadier general on the retired list, April 23, 1904. Toward the end of his life, Dr. Heger became blind. He died in Washington, D.C. about 1908.

GEORGE W. CARR

George W. Carr, who was Captain Archer's dear friend and first lieutenant at Simcoe, "went South," too, and became a Confederate colonel. He was captured on September 25, 1864, following the battle of Fisher's Hill.

"Among the prisoners," says Sheridan in his *Personal Memoirs*, "was a tall and fine looking officer, much worn with hunger and fatigue. The moment I saw him I recognized him as a former comrade, George W. Carr, with whom I had served in Washington Territory. He was in those days a lieutenant in the Ninth Infantry, and was one of the officers who superintended the execution of the nine Indians at the Cascades of the Columbia in 1856. Carr was very much emaciated, and greatly discouraged by the turn events recently had taken. For old acquaintance sake I gave him plenty to eat, and kept him in comfort at my headquarters until the next batch of prisoners was sent to the rear, when he went with them. He had resigned from the regular army at the commencement of hostilities, and, full of high anticipation, cast his lot with the Confederacy, but when he fell into our hands, his bright dreams having been dispelled by the harsh realities of war, he appeared to think that for him there was no future."

EDWARD J. STEPTOE

Edward Jevnor Steptoe, of Virginia, 1837 Academy graduate, second lieutenant, Third Artillery, served in the Florida War of 1838, and among the Cherokees while moving the Indians to the West. Infantry instructor at West Point, first lieutenant, Third Artillery, 1838; in the war with Mexico, he was promoted to captain for gallant and meritorious conduct in the battle for the capital city, and to major and to lieutenant colonel. In 1849-50 he was engaged in new Florida hostilities. In 1854-55 he was on the march to Washington Territory via Salt Lake City with an appointment as governor of Utah Territory, which he declined. He was appointed major of the Ninth Infantry, in garrison at Fort Monroe, on March 3, 1855, and had frontier duty at Fort Vancouver in '56. Engaged in the defense of the Cascades, March 27-28, 1856, he took part in the Yakima expedition, 1856, served in 1856-58 at Fort Walla Walla, and was on the Spokane expedition, 1858, against hostile Indians, defeated in the desperate combat of To-hots-nim-me, May 17. He was appointed lieutenant colonel of the Tenth Infantry, September 9, 1861. On sick leave, 1858-61, he resigned the service, November 1, 1861. He died at age 49 near Lynchburg, Virginia.

FREDERICK TRACY DENT

Frederick Tracy Dent (1820-92), another of the Simcoe officers who attained stature in the Civil War, was born in White Haven, Missouri. Ulysses S. Grant, his West Point classmate and also roommate for one year, there met Miss Julia Dent, who became Mrs. Grant. Dent was graduated from the Academy in 1843. With the Fifth Infantry in the battles of Contreras, Churubusco and Molino del Rey, he was successively breveted first lieutenant and captain for gallant and meritorious conduct. At Molino del Rey he received a musket ball in the thigh. His captaincy in the Ninth began March 3, 1855. He became a major in the Fourth Infantry and was breveted lieutenant colonel for gallant and meritorious conduct in the Battle of the Wilderness, and in 1865 won the brevet of brigadier general of volunteers, again for gallant and meritorious service. In 1870 he was transferred as lieutenant colonel, in the regular Army, to the Fifth Artillery.

DICKINSON WOODRUFF

Dickinson Woodruff, of Trenton, New Jersey, accepted his appointment as captain in the Ninth Infantry on March 22, 1855, at the age of 37 years. He was at Fort Simcoe and on escort duty with the Northwest Boundary Commission. Serving through the Civil War, he attained the rank of major in the Twenty-first Infantry. On March 26, 1868, he was promoted to lieutenant colonel of his original regiment, the Ninth, and was retired on December 15, 1870.

WILLIAM MYERS

William Myers, Pennsylvania, July 1, 1854 graduate of the Academy, brevet second lieutenant, Fifth Infantry, served with the Fourth, 1853-54, at Forts Belknap and McIntosh, Texas, briefly at Fort Dalles in early 1855. Ninth Infantry second lieutenant, March 3, 1855, he recruited for the newly reactivated regiment, and at Fort Simcoe, 1856-57, received promotion to first lieutenant. For about two years he had a hitch with the Coast Survey, followed by commissary and quartermaster duty at Fort Dalles. During the Rebellion he served at St. Louis in the Department of the Missouri, was promoted through the grades, breveted brigadier general of U.S. Volunteers and to like rank in the U.S. Army, March 13, 1865. Post-war service included the Department of the Platte, 1866-70, the San Francisco and Chicago depots, Department of Dakota, Department of California. On the occasion of a Japanese cultural mission visit to the United States in 1872 President Grant appointed Myers to provide for the comfort of the embassy and attached him as military aide to the prince in charge. Upon his retirement from active service, 1883, after 30 years in uniform he was deputy quartermaster general. He died November 11, 1887, in New York City, at the age of 57.

JOSEPH K. F. MANSFIELD

West Pointer from Connecticut and second in the class of 1822, Joseph K. F. Mansfield was of the elite in the Army's Corps of Engineers. As staff colonel, inspector general's department, he officiated at the Ninth Infantry's departure for the Yakima War in Washington Territory, where he conducted inspection again on the return of the troops from the campaign.

Ten years after promotion from graduate to second lieutenant, he was a first lieutenant, and six years later a captain. Forts, harbor defenses and river improvements largely occupied him until the war with Mexico. He was chief engineer of the Army under Maj. Gen. Zachary Taylor, 1846-47. For gallant and distinguished services in the defense of Fort Brown, Texas, which he constructed, he was breveted major. He was severely wounded while directing the storming of the Tannery Redoubt at Monterrey. For gallant and meritorious conduct in the several conflicts at Monterrey he was breveted lieutenant colonel. For like praiseworthy conduct in the battle of Buena Vista, February 22-23, 1847, he was breveted colonel.

Colonel, staff and inspector general, he served in the Departments of New Mexico, California, Texas, 1853-54, and in the Departments of Oregon and California, 1858-59.

Early in the Civil War he mustered volunteers at Columbus, Ohio, successively commanded the Department of Washington and the City of Washington, being breveted in May, 1861, to brigadier general and to full brigadier. He took part in the capture of Norfolk and Suffolk, Virginia, and July 18, 1862, was major general, U.S. Volunteers, commanding a divison of the Army of the Potomac in the Maryland campaign. In the battle of Antietam, "at the head of his troops, with sword waving over his head, cheering on his men to victory," he was mortally wounded and died the next day, September 18, 1862, aged 59.

PHILIP H. SHERIDAN

Philip Henry Sheridan (1831-88) was a natural fighter, ready-made for the path of glory, whereon his feet were planted when he was graduated from the United States Military Academy on July 1, 1853. He would have been with the class of '52 but for fisticuffs with a cadet sergeant, which cost him a year's suspension. His parents were second cousins, both from County Cavan, and Phil, the third child of six, was born in Albany, New York, the year after their arrival from Ireland. He grew up in Ohio and was appointed from that state to the Academy. For dash and daring, Sheridan was surpassed by none. Wherever he rode, men followed gladly. On the roll of Union generals, the names of Grant, Sherman and Sheridan lead all the rest, and

Sheridan's shines with no less effulgence than the others. His soldierly qualities were early displayed on the Texas frontier and in the Pacific Northwest. It was inevitable that he would succeed Sherman to the command of the Army upon the latter's retirement in 1883.

EDWARD OTHO CRESAP ORD

Edward Otho Cresap Ord (1818-83), born in Cumberland, Maryland, became one of the Union Army's most distinguished officers. Graduated from West Point in 1839 and commissioned second lieutenant, Third Artillery, he served in the Seminole War, 1839-42. During the Mexican War he performed garrison duty at Monterey, California. He was promoted to captain in 1850. He was with Colonel Wright in the battles of Four Lakes and Spokane Plains in 1858. He took part in the capture of John Brown at Harper's Ferry by Lt. Col. Robert E. Lee, October 17, 1859. Upon the outbreak of the Civil War, Ord was commissioned brigadier general of volunteers, and throughout the conflict held important commands. For gallantry at the capture of Fort Harrison, September 20, 1864, where he was severely wounded, he was breveted major general in the regular Army. After his recovery, he was given command of the Army of Virginia. Due in great part to Ord's skill and energy, Lee's retreating troops were headed off and compelled to surrender. General Sherman said that Ord's "skillful, hard march the night before was one of the chief causes of Lee's surrender." Ord was commissioned a brigadier general in 1866 and in 1881, a year after his retirement, major general by an act of Congress.

GEORGE CROOK

George Crook (1828-90), Ohio farm boy and West Point class of 1852, often was called the best Indian fighter of them all. He also was one of the best friends the Indians ever had. He deplored injustices done to them, interceded for them with civil and military authorities, and strove to right specific and grievous wrongs. He had a distinguished record in the Civil War, from which he emerged a major general, and subsequently won acclaim for his hard campaigning against the Apaches and the Sioux. Experience gained as a young lieutenant in the Rogue

River War and with the Yakima expedition of 1858 gave him a deep understanding of Indian nature and contributed to his larger successes on the frontiers.

HENRY M. JUDAH

Henry M. Judah, native of Maryland and a West Point graduate of 1843, was a brevet second lieutenant, Eighth Infantry, in the military occupation of Texas, 1845-46, and served with the Fourth Infantry in the Mexican War. For gallant and meritorious conduct in the battle of Molino del Rey he was breveted first lieutenant, and won a captain's brevet on a like citation following the battle of Chapultepec. Shortly after the assault and capture of Mexico City he was appointed first lieutenant. At Fort Vancouver in 1853 he was promoted to captain in the Fourth. His Pacific Coast service, 1853-61, included scouting in the vicinity of Fort Jones, California, temporary command of Fort Simcoe during Garnett's 1858 expedition, and subsequent duty at Fort Vancouver, Fort Steilacoom, and Fort Yuma, California. In September of 1861 he was made colonel of the Fourth California Volunteers and in December was assigned to the defenses of the national capital. On March 21, 1862, he was appointed brigadier general of U.S. Volunteers and had command of a division in the advance upon the seige of Corinth, Mississippi. He was promoted to major in the Fourth Infantry, June 30, 1862. In Sherman's "March from Atlanta to the Sea," Major Judah commanded the second division of the Twenty-third Corps. He died at Plattsburg Barracks, New York, January 14, 1866, at the age of 45.

HENRY M. BLACK

Henry Moorehouse Black, Pennsylvanian and 1847 graduate of the Academy, gave 51 years of devoted service to the infantry. Lieutenant in the Fourth, captain in the Ninth, major in the Seventh, lieutenant colonel of the Fourth and the Eighteenth regiments, and colonel of the Twenty-third, he was retired at Fort Sam Houston, Texas, January 15, 1891. In addition, he was colonel of the Sixth California Volunteer Infantry in 1863-64, and commandant of cadets and instructor of artillery, infantry and cavalry tactics at West Point from September 22, 1864, to

July 1, 1870. Following the abandonment of Fort Simcoe, he was stationed at Fort Dalles, 1859-61, and was in command of Fort Vancouver, June to November, 1861. In California his assignments included command of the Alcatraz Island military prison and command of the District of Humboldt during operations against hostile Indians. Colonel Black died August 5, 1893, in Chicago, at the age of 67, and was buried in the National Cemetery at Arlington.

HENRY DOUGLASS

Henry Douglass, of New York State, whose father, Maj. David B. Douglass, was professor of engineering at the Military Academy, was an 1852 graduate of that institution. His early service with the Seventh and Eighth Infantry regiments in Arkansas, Indian Territory and Texas—convoying wagon trains and scouting against Indians—inured him to the vicissitudes of the frontier before he came to Simcoe. His second lieutenancy in the Ninth dated from March 3, 1855, on the constitution of that regiment, in which he became a first lieutenant on September 19, 1856. He was principal assistant professor of drawing at the Academy, January 16, 1858, to July 2, 1861. Appointed captain in the Eighteenth Infantry, May 14, 1861, he saw action in many of the larger battles of the Civil War, beginning with Bull Run. For gallant and meritorious service at the battle of Murfreesboro, where he was wounded, Douglass won a major's brevet. On July 28, 1866, he was appointed major in the Third Infantry.

JOHN W. FRAZER

John W. Frazer, native of Tennessee, was appointed to the Academy from Mississippi and began his cadetship July 1, 1845. He was graduated on July 1, 1849, and promoted to brevet second lieutenant, Second Infantry. His first western duty was in California in 1850, at San Miguel and Benicia, and at Camp Far West, 1851 to 1855. He was in garrison at Fort Monroe, Virginia, in 1855, and on recruiting service, 1855-56. On appointment to the Ninth Infantry, March 3, 1855, he was promoted to first lieutenant of Company G, and, upon completing his recruiting duty, joined his company at Fort Simcoe on November

Later photo of Col. Henry Moorehouse Black, who was captain of Company G, Ninth Infantry, while at Fort Simcoe. (National Archives.)

2, 1856, relieving Lieut. Henry Douglass. On May 1, 1857, he was promoted to captain and assumed command of Company C on June 26. In 1859-60 he was on duty at Fort Colville. He resigned from the Army on March 15, 1861, and joined in the rebellion against the United States, gaining command of a brigade. In charge of the defense of Cumberland Gap, between Virginia and Tennessee, he surrendered without resistance on September 9, 1863, and 2,000 of his men were taken prisoners. Frazer was accused of cowardice but President Jefferson Davis believed that was an unjust allegation. After the war Frazer was a merchant and planter at Memphis.

JESSE K. ALLEN

Jesse K. Allen, of Hillsboro, Montgomery County, Illinois, was a native of Tennessee. Appointed to the Military Academy from Illinois, he was a cadet from September 1, 1851, to July 1, 1855. On graduation, he was promoted to brevet second lieutenant of infantry, and served in garrison at Fort Columbus, New York, and at Fort Monroe, Virginia, where he was advanced to second lieutenant in the Ninth Infantry on October 16, 1855. He was 28 years of age when he was killed on the Upper Yakima in August, 1858.

ELISHA E. CAMP

Elisha E. Camp, a native of New York, was second lieutenant in the Third Dragoons during the Mexican War. He resigned from the Army after the war. He accepted his second lieutenancy in the Ninth Infantry at Fort Simcoe in May 1857. Promoted to first lieutenant in May, 1861, and on the following August 3 to captain, he served as assistant quartermaster under Lt. Col. Rufus Ingalls in Washington, D.C. He died in the capital on August 4, 1867.

JAMES B. S. ALEXANDER

James B. S. Alexander, Virginian and an 1856 graduate of the Academy, had a short career. In garrison at Carlisle Barracks, Pennsylvania, he received promotion to second lieutenant, Ninth Infantry, September 10, 1856. He served at Simcoe, 1857-59, at Fort Dalles, 1859-60, was on leave of absence, 1860-61, and resigned on May 9, 1861. He died, 1861, at Charlottesville, Virginia, aged 25.

SOURCES

PUBLISHED

Bancroft, Hubert H. *History of Oregon*, Vol. 2. The History Co., San Francisco, 1888. Also *History of Washington, Idaho, and Montana.* The History Co., San Francisco, 1890.

Chestnut, Mary B. *A Diary From Dixie*. Edited by Ben A. Williams. Houghton Mifflin Co., Boston, 1949.

Chisholm, William G. "The Garnetts of Essex County and Their Homes," *Virginia Historical Magazine of History and Biography*, 42 (1934), 2-4, 166-80, 256-68, 358-66.

Crook, George. *General George Crook: His Autobiography*. Edited by Martin F. Schmitt. University of Oklahoma Press, Norman, 1946.

Cullum, Brevet Major-General George W. *Biographical Register of the Officers and Graduates of the U.S. Military Academy*, Vol. 1, rev. ed., 1879; Vol. 2, 1868.

Downing, Andrew Jackson. *Architecture of Country Houses; Including Designs for Cottages, Farmhouses, and Villas*. New York, 1857.

Freeman, Douglas S. *Lee's Lieutenants*. Charles Scribner's Sons, New York, 1944.

Glisan, Rodney. *Journal of Army Life*. A. L. Bancroft & Co., San Francisco, 1874.

Grant, Ulysses S. *Personal Memoirs of U. S. Grant*. Charles L. Webster & Co., New York, 1885.

Keyes, E. D. *Fifty Years Observation of Men and Events, Civil and Military*. Charles Scribner's Sons, New York, 1884.

Knuth, Priscilla. *"Picturesque" Frontier: The Army's Fort Dalles*. Oregon Historical Society, Portland, [1967].

Lerwill, Lieut. Col. Leonard L. *The Personnel Replacement System in the United States Army*. Department of the Army Pamphlet No. 20-211 [Washington, D.C.], 1954.

McClellan, George B. *McClellan's Own Story*. Charles Webster & Co., New York, 1887.

McWhorter, Lucullus V. *Tragedy of the Wahk-shum*. Privately printed, Yakima, 1937.

Meany, Edmond S. *History of the State of Washington*. Macmillan Co., New York, 1909.

Mills, Randall V. *Stern-Wheelers Up Columbia*. Pacific Books, Palo Alto, 1947.

Moore, Frank, ed. *The Rebellion Record*. G. P. Putnam, New York, 1863. Vol. 2, pp. 288-96 (Cincinnati *Gazette*, Cincinnati *Commercial*, etc.)

The Photographic History of the Civil War (10 vols.). The Review of Reviews Co., New York, 1911.

Russell, William H. *My Diary North and South*. Edited by Fletcher Pratt. Harper & Brothers, New York, 1954.

Scholl, Louis. "Recollections of Sixty Years," *Up-to-the-Times Magazine* (Walla Walla, Wn.), October 1907-January 1908.

Sheridan, Philip H. *Personal Memoirs of P. H. Sheridan,* Charles L. Webster & Co., New York, 1888.
Snowden, Clinton H. *A History of Washington,* Vols. 3 and 4. The Century History Co., New York, 1909.
Splawn, A. J. *Ka-mi-akin, the Last Hero of the Yakimas.* Portland, 1917.
Stevens, Hazard. *The Life of Isaac Ingalls Stevens.* Houghton Mifflin Co., 1900.
U. S. Army. Adjutant General's Office. *General Orders* 1866, 1868, 1870. Government Printing Office, Washington, D.C.
U. S. Congress. *Senate Executive Document No. 78. Reports of Explorations and Surveys to Ascertain the . . . Route for a Railroad from the Mississippi River to the Pacific Ocean.* Vol. 1. Government Printing Office, Washington, D.C., 1855. Also *Reports of the Secretary of War,* Dec. 3, 1855; 1856-57; Dec. 6, 1858; 1860.
Victor, Frances Fuller. *The Early Indian Wars of Oregon.* F.C. Baker, Salem, 1894.
The War of the Rebellion: A Compilation of the Official Records of the Union and Confederate Armies. Series 1, Vol. 2. Government Printing Office, 1880.

UNPUBLISHED

Archer, James J., Papers. Maryland Historical Society, Baltimore. [TS copy, Click Relander, Yakima.]
Chisholm, William Garnett, Papers. Leesburg, Virginia. [Includes Robert Selden Garnett's military record, endorsed by himself.]
Fort Simcoe Guard Reports. Yakima Valley Museum, Yakima.
Garnett, Marianna, Letters. In the possession of G. P. Bainbridge, Vancouver, B.C.
National Archives, Washington, D.C. Assorted U.S. Army records, including: War Department, Letters Received, 1854-59; Fort Simcoe Post Returns; Records of U.S. Army Commands, Dept. of Pacific, 1856-58; "Annual Return of the Alterations and Casualties incident to the 9th Regiment of Infantry commanded by Col. George Wright during the year 1858," and Major R.S. Garnett's Special Report, Sept. 18, 1856 (on death of Captain Bowman); other records, including post inspections in RG 94, Adjutant General's Office.
Scholl, Louis. Application for pension, Feb. 1, 1906. (Author's collection.)

ACKNOWLEDGEMENTS

For much of the official Army material drawn on for this book the author is indebted to Leonard L. Lerwill, of Yakima, Lieutenant Colonel, Infantry, United States Army. While engaged in research for historical works he contemplated writing about his native Oregon and the Pacific Northwest, Colonel Lerwill took valuable time to dig into files in Washington, D.C., for documents bearing on Fort Simcoe and the Yakima War. He also gathered material from the personal files of the late William Garnett Chisholm, at Leesburg, Virginia.

Colonel Lerwill's capacity for scholarly research and sound writing is revealed in his *The Personnel Replacement System in the United States Army* (Dept. of Army pamphlet No. 20-211, August, 1954). This exhaustive volume, first of the kind, covers the subject of military manpower marshaling from the Colonial Period to the close of World War II.

Colonel Lerwill met his death in Korea, in a land mine accident, December 10, 1955.

With Colonel Lerwill, this writer visited the "Garnett country" in Essex County, Virginia, where the several branches of the family had large antebellum estates, and where one, Elmwood, remains in the possession of Mr. Muscoe R. H. Garnett, of New York City. Together, Colonel Lerwill and the author, in May, 1953, toured the old northwestern Virginia region wherein the Union and Confederate forces clashed in 1861, and viewed the field where General Garnett died, at Carrick's Ford, Parsons, West Virginia.

Helpful in assembling the material were: Louis Scholl, Jr., The Dalles, Ore.; Mrs. Charles D. Shane, Lick Observatory, Mt. Hamilton, Calif.; Z. F. Moody, Portland; Click Relander, Yakima; Mrs. Mary Ethel Swanstrom, Seattle; The Hon. O. H. "Hal" Holmes, Ellensburg and Washington, D.C.; Howard Sedgwick, Silver Spring, Md.; Mrs. G. W. Miller, secretary, The Unitarian Church of All Souls, New York; William Garnett Chisholm, Leesburg, Va.; Muscoe R. H. Garnett, New York; Theodore S. Garnett, Norfolk, Va.; Charles L. Garnett, Columbus, Miss.; Mrs. Goldie Garnett Wallace, Visalia, Calif.; First Lieut. Harry M. Hunke, Jr., Infantry, public information officer, Fort Lewis, Wn.; Dr. Sidney Forman, archivist, United States Military Academy; W. Neil Franklin, chief, National Archives and Records Service, General Services Administration; Robert E. Grayson, director, editorial library, New York *Herald Tribune;* Dr. Wilbur L. Hall, state librarian, Virginia State Library; Olaf T. Hagen, research technician, National Park Service; Priscilla Knuth, Oregon Historical Society; G. P. Bainbridge, Vancouver, B.C.; Mrs. J. J. Bartholet, Yakima; Ben B. Olney (grandson of Capt. Nathan Olney and who long resided at the military road crossing on Toppenish Creek, at the Haller battlefield); George Umtuch, Kiutus Jim, and Alex Saluskin, Yakima Indian tribal leaders; Otto K. Rightmire, Parsons, W.Va.; John Kenney, mayor, Parsons, W. Va. Director Thomas Vaughan and other Historical Society staff members, including Bruce T. Hamilton and Maurice Hodge, with Donald P. Abbott and Mrs. Richard Godfrey, have aided in the production of the enlarged second edition.

INDEX

Fort Simcoe appears in about the center of the map, which shows roads and access to park and museum, buildings and pleasant picnic grounds. So far off regular transportation routes and in use as Indian agency, much more survived from the fort's original construction, more than a century and a quarter ago, than at many frontier posts. (Washington State Highway Commission).